MARCHIN' THE PILGRIMS HOME

Contributions to the Study of Religion
Series Editor: Henry W. Bowden

Private Churches and Public Money: Church-Government Fiscal Relations
Paul J. Weber and Dennis A. Gilbert

A Cultural History of Religion in America
James G. Moseley

Religious Mythology and the Art of War: Comparative Religious Symbolisms of Military Violence
James A. Aho

Saints, Slaves, and Blacks: The Changing Place of Black People Within Mormonism
Newell G. Bringhurst

Southern Anglicanism: The Church of England in Colonial South Carolina
S. Charles Bolton

The Cult Experience
Andrew J. Pavlos

Southern Enterprize: The Work of National Evangelical Societies in the Antebellum South
John W. Kuykendall

Facing the Enlightenment and Pietism: Archibald Alexander and the Founding of Princeton Theological Seminary
Lefferts A. Loetscher

Presbyterian Women in America: Two Centuries of a Quest for Status
Lois A. Boyd and R. Douglas Brackenridge

MARCHIN'
THE PILGRIMS
HOME

Leadership and
Decision-Making in an
Afro-Caribbean Faith

STEPHEN D. GLAZIER

CONTRIBUTIONS TO THE STUDY OF RELIGION,
NUMBER 10

GREENWOOD PRESS

WESTPORT, CONNECTICUT ● LONDON, ENGLAND

Library of Congress Cataloging in Publication Data

Glazier, Stephen D.
  Marchin' the pilgrims home.

  (Contributions to the study of religion, ISSN 0196-
7053 ; no. 10)
  Bibliography: p.
  Includes index.
  1. Baptists—Trinidad. 2. Trinidad—Religious life
and customs. 3. Blacks—Trinidad—Religion. I. Title.
II. Series.
BX6266.T74G55   1983   286'.5   82-24179
ISBN 0-313-23464-7 (lib. bdg.)

Library of Congress Catalog Card Number: 82-24179
ISBN: 0-313-23464-7
ISSN: 0196-7053

First published in 1983

Greenwood Press
A division of Congressional Information Service, Inc.
88 Post Road West
Westport, Connecticut 06881

Printed in the United States of America

10 9 8 7 6 5 4 3 2 1

To my wife Rosemary

March, march, the pilgrims home
We will march, march, the pilgrims home
We will march, march, the pilgrims home
To the new Jerusalem.

Spiritual Baptist hymn often sung at the conclusion of the mourning ceremony. Travel is a central concept in the faith, but while Baptist eyes may be on the "new Jerusalem," their feet are firmly planted in the here and now.

• Contents

● Illustrations

• *Tables*

• Series Foreword

IN THE first half of this century, a number of observers noted a Caribbean religious group variously referred to as Shouters, Shakers, Shango Baptists, or Spiritual Baptists. Such passing references did not serve participants well and may have misled researchers to concentrate on marginal aspects of the religion.

The author of this volume seeks to correct such misinterpretations by focusing on central values that make this particular group important for religious studies in general. An estimated ten thousand Spiritual Baptists, as group members prefer to be known, live on Trinidad, and Professor Glazier has provided the fullest ethnography and most sophisticated analysis to date of their faith. Building upon earlier hypotheses developed by Melville and Frances Herskovits, Roger Bastide, and George Eaton Simpson, Glazier has been able to assess the religion in light of firsthand data gathered in the field. Now that we have a greater knowledge of distinguishing Spiritual Baptist beliefs and rituals, we can appreciate more fully how these churches function as institutions.

Between 1976 and 1982, Professor Glazier amassed data on 240 members of Spiritual Baptist churches on Trinidad. He utilized 3 principal informants and interviewed 45 officials while also photographing and recording worship services. He conveys data about Sunday worship, funerals, thanksgiving feasts, and curing sessions with both the empathy of a participant and the objectivity of a field observer. The most important rituals he witnessed were baptisms, mourning ceremonies, and pilgrimages, and Glazier's reflections on those activities give this work its distinctive factual grounding. After describing the group's myths and belief system as well as its prominent symbols and rituals, he proceeds to explain Spiritual Baptists in light of social, economic, political, and even geographical circumstances. The key to understanding them, he finds, is local leadership, the exercise of personal influence directed primarily through economic channels and developed over time to something approaching a *de facto* hierarchical institution without the sanction of *de jure* legitimization.

This fresh examination of actual practices causes us to reconsider some earlier impressions of Afro-American religion, many of them drawn from experiences outside the Caribbean region. Glazier shows once again that the old, European-based typology of church, sect, and cult is truly outmoded when applied to phenomena in the western hemisphere. He points out that spirit possession is not the strongest feature of Spiritual Baptists, and it does not function primarily to enhance ego or status among poor blacks on the island. The fact that churches attract wealthy blacks, creoles, and East Indians challenges theories of sublimation for marginal classes. The faith combines elements of Hinduism, Islam, and Buddhism plus strong emphasis on Christianity and African tribal religions. Such composites require a new look at theories of syncretism because modern conditions of religious freedom, mobility, and rivalry indicate a process of differentiation alongside doctrinal conflation. Glazier finds that African retentions are not a central characteristic of Spiritual Baptists. Their churches do retain African roots, but that is only part of a complex whole, subject to more dominant concerns about survival in a modern capitalist economy.

Spiritual Baptist churches are not egalitarian in the sense of careers open to talents or even spiritual experience. There are twenty–two ranks to leadership offices, and the motivation to rise in the hierarchy is strong. But there is no regular correspondence between an individual's spiritual capacity and advancement in rank. Leaders advance only when others above them allow that person to approximate their own level. The principal qualities looked for do not support the old Weberian notion of personal charisma but rather give preference to financial acumen and antagonism to uncontrolled ecstasy. Glazier's study indicates that there is considerable diversity among local religious leaders. They make independent decisions about beliefs and practices along a spectrum of conservative and innovative options. But leaders as a whole tend to stress economic stability, routinized liturgies, and successful recruitment as keys to ecclesiastical success. These features place Spiritual Baptists in a setting where management techniques and the development of institutionalized authority may be as important as the question of African tribal variants.

Henry W. Bowden

● *Preface*

A PRIMARY goal of this book is to provide an ethnography of the Spiritual Baptists in Trinidad. Although much has been written on this religion, both in Trinidad and the United States, many gaps can be found in the ethnographic record.

In planning my research, I felt that there was need to focus on this religion in terms of leadership decisions within their institutional settings. Such a study has not been attempted previously. This may reflect what M. G. Smith has termed the "anti-institutional bias" in Caribbean studies.[1] A major thrust of this study will be to show that Baptist churches must be seen as institutions. Many have been in continuous operation for over fifty years and have developed very complex bureaucracies, a polity, and even what might be termed "church law." These churches face problems of recruitment, budget, personnel, and succession to high office similar to those problems faced by institutions the world over. Attention must be given to institutional settings, because without such attention studies of a religion are at best incomplete.

Previous researchers treated the Spiritual Baptists as a variant of tribal religions in Africa.[2] The difficulty with this approach is that Caribbean religions differ dramatically from those of tribal peoples. A major distinction is that Caribbean religions face problems of recruitment and financing seldom encountered in a tribal setting. Also, in the plural societies of the Caribbean, individuals choose to participate in a given religion from among hundreds of possible choices, and one's religious life is separated to a large extent from one's other concerns. Ethnic affiliation and religious belief are no longer coterminous.

My interest in leadership decisions may reflect my experiences as a denominational minister in the United States. I found that I was able to identify with many of the problems faced by Baptist leaders in Trinidad and, in subsequent discussions of these problems, discovered that they provided a "key" to the inner workings of the church. Leadership decisions, as Barth postulated, are valuable ethnographic data.[3] By focusing on the decision-making process, the ethnographer gains a better understanding of cultural systems, especially if he or she is able to carry out research over a period of several years.

Research on the Baptists was conducted during the summers of 1976, 1977, 1978, and 1979. I visited briefly in the summer of 1982 and found that things had changed somewhat but that my earlier impressions were by and large correct. Whenever possible, I have tried to incorporate new data into this presentation. In all, I attended thirty-four major public ceremonies (Sunday worship, baptisms, mourning ceremonies, and pilgrimages), seven minor events (Thanksgivings held at private homes, funerals, Wednesday services, etc.), three Shango feasts, and three curing sessions. These services were held at twenty-four locations.

Because my research spanned a period of several years, it was possible for me to test and refine ideas about religious leadership. For example, I was able to observe the religious careers of several Baptist leaders and to predict, on the basis of my model, who would be a successful leader and who would not. Often my predictions held true, but sometimes I was forced to consider additional factors that I had neglected previously. With each successive year my "model" of religious leadership became stronger.

Observations of public worship contributed to my knowledge of church ritual and facilitated contact with church members. They also provided follow-up material for interviews conducted with twenty-eight leaders (nineteen males; nine females) and seventeen lower-ranking church members.

Extensive "life history" data gathered from three informants (two males; one female) provided insight into the internal workings of church organization and occasionally provided details that opened new avenues of research.

In all, I have compiled data on over 240 church members,

including information on rank, sex, and occupation. This sample represents almost all Baptists in the Curepe community.

Documentary evidence includes tape recordings of fourteen complete worship services (about forty hours), photographs, partial financial records for eighteen pilgrimages, information from papers on file in the library of the University of the West Indies, and information from the personal diaries of two prominent Baptist leaders.

The suburban community of Curepe (located about eight miles northeast of Port of Spain on the Eastern Main Road), served as the location for fieldwork during 1976 and 1978. Curepe is by no means the center of Baptist activity in Trinidad (if, indeed, there is a "center" at all). Curepe was chosen primarily because housing was available in the area. As it turned out, it would not have mattered greatly where I had chosen to live, since most Spiritual Baptists do not attend services in their own communities but prefer to go to church in neighboring towns. In 1977 and 1979 I lived on the campus of the University of the West Indies in St. Augustine, and in 1982, I lived briefly in a Port of Spain guesthouse.

Baptists in all three locations aided me in my research. In Curepe my nextdoor neighbor, Mother Rocke, was a high-ranking member of the Spiritual Baptist church in Las Lomas; in St. Augustine, I was assisted by a very active Baptist leader, Albert DeBique, who lived opposite my dormitory at the university. Both Baptists took me to their churches, introduced me to other church members, and otherwise attempted to foster my understanding of church "operations." If there are any shortcomings in this presentation, the blame does not rest with them. For their help, I express my heartfelt gratitude.

A majority of my Baptist informants are literate (although many older members of the faith cannot read), sophisticated, and both willing and able to speak for themselves. In writing this account, I have been very much aware that my findings will be discussed and criticized by members of the religion and that anthropologists no longer enjoy a monopoly on the act of interpretation. This is a very healthy situation and cannot help but have positive consequences for the discipline of anthropology as a whole.

Thanks are due to a number of people for their guidance and encouragement. I especially thank Professor Seth Leacock of the University of Connecticut, who read and commented on the several drafts of this essay; Professor Leslie G. Desmangles of Trinity College, Hartford; Mr. Archibald Singh and the late Andrew T. Carr of the National Culture Council of Trinidad and Tobago; Dr. Colleen Ward of the Institute of Social and Economic Research at the University of the West Indies; Professors Vincent Crapanzano and Hildred Geertz, both of whom have greatly influenced my anthropological thinking; and Professor Leonard Barrett, who recommended this study for publication.

P. I. Gomes of the University of the West Indies and Monica and Michael Charbonné of Maraval went out of their way to make my stays in Trinidad enjoyable.

Yale University facilitated my research by appointing me a Research Fellow for the academic year 1981-1982.

Betty Seaver typed several drafts of this study with patience and good humor.

As I write this, the people of Trinidad and Tobago make plans to celebrate their twentieth anniversary of Independence. I wish them my best.

Stephen D. Glazier
Port of Spain, Trinidad
August, 1982

MARCHIN' THE PILGRIMS HOME

• Introduction

TRINIDAD'S Spiritual Baptists are part of an international religious movement with congregations in Tobago, St. Vincent (where they are known as the Shakers), Grenada, Venezuela, Guyana (where they are known as the Jordanites), New York City, and Toronto. Earlier studies of the religion, notably those of Herskovits and Herskovits[1] and Simpson,[2] referred to the group as the Shouters, an appellation members neither use nor appreciate. Believers refer to their faith as the Spiritual Baptist church or, more commonly, as the Baptists.

I estimate that there are about ten thousand members of the Baptist faith in Trinidad.[3] Membership is predominantly black, and cuts across social and economic lines. Over the past ten years an increasing number of wealthy East Indians and creoles have become involved in the religion. Most churches are small; their memberships range from less than twenty to two hundred.

The Baptist faith is an amalgam of many beliefs and practices and has been greatly influenced by other religions on the island. Aspects of Baptist ritual are borrowed from the four major world religions (Christianity, Islam, Hinduism, and Buddhism) as well as from African-derived tribal religions. Christianity and African-derived religions seem to have had the greatest impact on the faith.

In the eyes of many believers, two rituals distinguish their religion from all other religions on the island: baptism and mourning ceremonies. Both of these rituals are considered central to the faith, as they play a part in determining one's church rank. Twenty-two separate ranks are recognized in each church, and specific duties and privileges are associated with each rank.

Most church members are strongly motivated to rise in the church hierarchy.

Many Trinidadians confuse the Baptists with a local African-derived cult group known as Shango (see Appendix). They lump Shango centers and Baptist churches under the rubric "Shango Baptists," and suppose that Baptist and Shango rituals are identical. One reason for this may be that the average Trinidadian has had little exposure to Baptist rites, and few take the trouble to find out what goes on during Baptist ceremonies.[4]

Baptist churches and Shango centers are separate; however, there are four types of relations that may exist between a Baptist church and a Shango center: (1) Baptist churches exist with no Shango connections, (2) Baptist churches exist with Shango connections, (3) Shango centers exist with no Baptist connections, and (4) Shango centers exist with Baptist connections. Membership in these faiths does overlap, and the above distinctions reflect ways in which believers think of themselves. Are they, for example, Baptists who also "do" Shango or Shangoists who also "do" Baptist rites?

Baptist and Shango rituals differ. Baptist rituals are directed to different gods than are Shango rituals. While Baptist rites are said to focus exclusively on their version of the Holy Trinity, Shango rites focus on "African" gods. Both Shangoists and Baptists are polytheists, but in the words of one informant, "Us Baptists does not worship them others."

The separation of "African," Christian, Islamic, Hindu, and other rites within the Baptist faith is not an easy task for the anthropologist, although leaders in the faith claim to experience little difficulty in classifying rites and are able to separate them by the principle of juxtaposition to be described in Chapter 3. The overwhelming majority of informants stated that they were "Christians because they reads the Bible and believes in the Trinity." Despite many differences between Baptist practices and those usually associated with Christianity, I have adopted their classification for some sections of my presentation. I might add that the history of Christianity grants considerable leeway as to what may be classified as Christian and what may not be so classified.

Earlier researchers of the Baptist faith have focused on the religion to substantiate hypotheses developed, for the most part, outside the Caribbean region. Herskovits, for example, conceived the religion as pivotal to his theories concerning cultural change and African retentions in the New World, and he sought to demonstrate "how this Baptist 'shouting' is a direct reinterpretation of the Shango cult."[5] For Herskovits and his followers, the Baptist church was simply a case study used to verify continuities between cultural traits of New World blacks and blacks of sub-Saharan Africa.

More recently, researchers have studied the Baptists as part of a worldwide survey of trance and possession states.[6] The church is an excellent laboratory for the study of possession states and altered states of consciousness because the Baptist faith recognizes three distinct types of possession behavior (glossolalia and/or possession by the Holy Ghost, possession by "African" gods in Shango rituals, and possession by "orisha" or evil spirits) as well as mourning rites, which earlier researchers interpreted as an example of altered states of consciousness induced by sensory deprivation.

These approaches concentrated on selected aspects of religious life (e.g., the mourning ceremony or so-called "Africanisms") often to the exclusion of other aspects. Little attention has been devoted to the religion as a whole.

My approach has been much more holistic. I will concentrate on leadership decisions and how they play a crucial role in almost every aspect of church life. Baptist leaders are powerful men who exert considerable authority over ambitious members of their own congregations, and their choices influence the faith as a whole.

Simpson, in his study of the faith, stated that the Baptist church was "egalitarian."[7] This contrasts with my findings and those of Henney, who observed on St. Vincent that "the freedom and autonomy that characterize each Shaker [Spiritual Baptist] group *vis-à-vis* other Shaker groups contrast sharply with the hierarchical structures and positive emphasis on obedience existing within each group. 'Obedience is the first step to Christ' and consequently each member is expected to obey those 'elder to him' in the group."[8] Many Baptist leaders in Trinidad exercise almost dictatorial control over members of their flock. There are, of course, also leaders who are less powerful.

The area in which leaders exert their greatest authority is that of church advancement. Previous analyses of the mourning ceremony have played down the impact of individual leadership decisions on the assignment of church rank and have also played down the significance of the rite for the perpetuation of churches as institutions.

Previous studies have implied that church advancement is directly related to altered states of consciousness experienced in the mourning room, but models stressing psychological experience do not account for actual observed patterns of church advancement. Between 1976 and 1982, many of my informants, otherwise ambitious and sincere, failed to advance, while seemingly less sincere brethren advanced rapidly. Many of these informants reported identical visions in the mourning room but did not advance equally within the faith. One reason for this is that church advancement is not based on one's visions per se, but on one's visions as they are interpreted by church leaders. My data indicate that there is no regular correspondence between a particular vision and a particular rank.

Wealth is an important factor in predicting rapid church advancement. In the mourning ceremony, I found that questions as to how much an individual could "contribute" to the church sometimes took precedence over individual merit and "spiritual readiness." Some individuals seemed to advance no matter what visions they received, while others lagged behind irrespective of their spiritual readiness. Baptists are very much aware of this and speak of it in terms of the "politics of mourning." Church leaders, in all cases, have the final say.

My treatment of the mourning ceremony differs from that of earlier works, and in some respects my conclusions are incompatible with the earlier conclusions of Simpson, Henney, Ward and Beaubrun, and Parks. Nevertheless, my conclusions are consistent with what sociologists of religion—especially those who have been influenced by Max Weber—call the process of "routinization." Institutional leaders, according to this theory, distrust ecstatic experience and, whenever possible, seek to control it. Ennis, in his survey of the literature, suggested that "societies in general, and institutions in particular, are reluctant to lose control over members and are especially ferocious toward anyone reaching directly for ecstasy by short-cutting proper channels."[9] Some Baptist leaders would claim that visions and dreams in the mourning room are sometimes false and cannot be trusted to perpetuate a viable religious organization and that this is why they struggle so ferociously to maintain their monopoly over church advancement.

Attention must be given to both male and female conceptions of church "operations." Many of my female informants, for example, professed to believe that church rank was determined by visions and dreams. Females stressed the importance of religious experience. Male informants, on the other hand, discounted the importance of religious experience and were much more cynical about church ritual. For most males, visions and dreams were seen as having little bearing on church advancement. On the basis of my observations, I believe that male assessments are accurate.

Differences of male and female attitudes may be found elsewhere in the culture. Trinidadian males have very different ideas concerning "respectability" than do Trinidadian females. For males, the way to become respectable is to dominate social institutions, while females can become respectable by merely participating in such institutions. Institutional leadership— whether fraternal, economic, political, or religious—is considered to be exclusively the domain of males. This does not mean, however, that women lack power. Among the Spiritual Baptists, it was emphasized repeatedly that male and female roles are complementary, that they "needs each other." A Baptist leader (male) cannot operate his church without a mother (female) and vice versa. What this does mean, however, is that females have very little to say about the day-to-day operations of their churches. Females have their own systems of rank and prestige.

The question of "unit of analysis" is also of tremendous theoretical importance. Research carried out in one community may present a somewhat biased view of the religion. In order to avoid such a bias, I followed my informants to services all over the island. Only three or four times did I attend a church in the community where I lived.

If one stays in one's own community, he or she will experience a religion as an "insider." If one follows one's informants to churches in other communities, he or she will experience the religion as an "outsider." Both perspectives can be valid; nevertheless, I agree with Michael Lieber that it is most fruitful to follow the flow of the action.[10] A majority of Baptists do experience their religion as outsiders. Spiritual Baptist churches may serve their communities, but they are not, strictly speaking, community churches.

Caribbean researchers, I believe, must begin to question the community study approach. Some of the best anthropological research in the Caribbean has been conducted in isolated areas (such as Toco), while a majority of Caribbean people live in urban and suburban areas. In Trinidad and Tobago, few areas are truly isolated; and by concentrating on the isolated areas, we may have greatly distorted Caribbean reality.

Ritual change is another area of church life where leadership decisions are important. While others, most notably Roger Bastide and Herskovits,[11] have explained ritual change in the New World as part of a global process of syncretism, ritual change in the Baptist case may also be understood in terms of a decision-making model. Leaders choose which rituals to add and when to add them.

Bastide correctly noted that whenever two or more religious traditions exist in proximity, there is sometimes a tendency for them to merge. There is another, opposing, tendency for these traditions to become further differentiated. The study of Caribbean religions has focused on the former process often to the exclusion of the latter. In Baptist ritual both differentiation and merging were noted; however, the processes of ritual differentiation were by far the more pronounced. In Trinidad, where once there had been evidence for a blending of African and Christian traditions,[12] separation had become dominant. Rituals once practiced in close proximity (e.g., Baptist services and Shango) are now carried out in different buildings and, whenever possible, in different communities. For example, chromolithographs of saints, once prevalent in Shango, have been removed from most Shango centers.

In the twenty-year gap between Simpson's fieldwork and my own, dramatic changes have occurred in Trinidadian society.

Those changes that may relate to ritual differentiation are increased mobility, greater religious freedom, and a concomitant increase in rivalry among religious leaders. Cumont found that in third-century Rome religious syncretism was related to periods of religious persecution and limited mobility and that differentiation was related to periods of religious freedom and mobility.[13] Similar forces may have determined the forms of ritual change in the Spiritual Baptist church.

I. M. Lewis classified the Spiritual Baptists as a "peripheral cult," and stated that the religion consists of low-status women (and men) seeking to improve their underprivileged position in Trinidadian society.[14] He also suggested that the religion serves as an oblique form of protest against the established order. The Baptists, according to Lewis, are acceptable to the established order only when they present themselves as part of a curing cult or operate clandestinely.

Much of what Lewis asserted about the Baptists and other Caribbean religions may have been true twenty years ago, but it is no longer applicable. The Baptists, as will be shown, do not present themselves as part of a curing cult (curing, in fact, is deemphasized); nor do they operate in a manner that could in any way be considered clandestine. It may be more useful to look at the Baptists (and other area religions) within their societal contexts. The Baptists are no longer peripheral, and should be seen as an integral part of Trinidadian society; they are no longer an institution separated from the economic, social, and political life of the island.

Lewis based these statements on research conducted in Trinidad when Trinidad was something of a backwater. Since that time, Trinidad has become a fairly prosperous nation, and the Spiritual Baptists have shared in its prosperity. One of the goals of my research has been to examine the consequences of affluence for a religious group whose primary appeal had previously been among the poor. What happens when a "religion of the oppressed" joins the establishment? Such studies of a religion are rare in the sociological literature and are nonexistent for the Caribbean.

Bastide divided all Afro-American religions into two groups.[15] Some religions, like Brazilian Candomblé and Cuban Santeria, are said to be *en conserve*, while other religions, like Haitian vodun, are said to be *vivantes*. The former, according to Bastide, represent a kind of defense mechanism or "cultural fossilization"—a fear that any small change may bring disastrous consequences; the latter religions are more secure in themselves and are freer to adapt to the changing needs of their clientele.

Baptist leaders are very conservative in their attempts to preserve or maintain some aspects of ritual form. On the other hand, Baptist leaders are also innovative in their adoption of rituals from many religious traditions, and no two Baptist services are ever exactly the same. In my fieldwork, I noted both fossilization and dynamism. For this reason I am not certain that it would be possible, or particularly fruitful, to classify the Baptist faith as either *en conserve* or *vivantes*.

Price contends that "tenacious fidelity to 'African' forms is, in many cases, an indication of a culture having finally lost meaningful touch with the vital African past."[16] The same could be said for tenacious fidelity to any ritual form and no Spiritual Baptist church in Trinidad could be accused of such tenacious fidelity.

Before discussing leadership, the next two chapters will deal with the setting of the Spiritual Baptist church and a discussion of the Baptist belief system. Chapter 3 will provide a description of major church rituals and examine leadership roles as they relate to ritual change. In Chapter 4, I will turn to church organization and deal with the role of leaders in promoting candidates for high church office. Chapter 5 will assess the leader's impact on church economics, with special attention to decisions concerning fund raising and expenditures. In Chapter 6, I will offer some conclusions as to the nature of leadership within the Baptist tradition and summarize the importance of leadership decisions for the church as a whole. An Appendix will contain a description of Shango ceremonies for comparative purposes.

1 • The Setting

TRINIDAD, the southernmost of the West Indian islands, lies immediately opposite the delta of the Orinoco River and occupies an area of 1,863 square miles. The island was discovered by Columbus on his third voyage to the New World in 1498, when he took possession in the name of the Spanish Crown. The Spanish, however, showed little interest in the island, and the first attempt at colonization was not until 1533 when Antonio Sedeño, who had been appointed Captain-General of Trinidad, established a small fort there. Sedeño's fort was soon abandoned, and the next serious attempt at settlement was in 1592 when Don Antonio de Berrio y Oruña founded the town of St. Joseph. De Berrio hoped to use Trinidad as a stepping-stone to the mainland and to the legendary city of gold, El Dorado.

For nearly three hundred years of Spanish rule, Trinidad was something of a backwater. Things changed somewhat when in 1797 the Spanish garrison on the island was defeated by British forces under Sir Ralph Abercrombie. In 1802, the island was ceded to the Crown of Great Britain by the Treaty of Amiens.

Island aborigines (Carinapagotos, Arawaks, Salvaios, Sepuyos, and Yaos) at the time of contact disappeared rapidly because of Spanish (and Carib) slave raids and the influx of European disease.[1] This led to severe labor shortages, and in 1783 the Spanish governor opened Trinidad to settlers from other islands. At this time a number of white planters from Martinique, Guadeloupe, Haiti (then Santo Domingo), and other Catholic islands arrived, along with their slaves. Their descendants have influenced the culture greatly, and some areas of the parish of

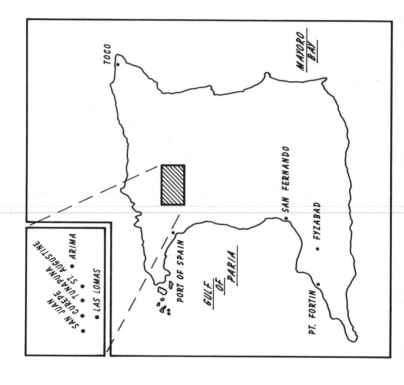

Figure 1. Map of Trinidad. Insert shows selected Spiritual Baptist centers.

St. George still boast pockets of speakers of French and Spanish. The Spanish spoken in the north-central region is a standard dialect, whereas Trinidadian French is a patois.

Under British rule, the number of black slaves increased, although some scholars have argued that slavery never was an important institution for the island economy.[2] A majority of Trinidad blacks migrated from other West Indian islands after emancipation in 1834.[3] Former slaves flocked to urban areas, and today many urban areas in Trinidad are predominantly black.

In the 1800s, a sizable number of immigrants came also from Madeira, the Azores, and parts of Europe and the United States. Those from Europe identified with the white upper classes, while those from the Azores and Madeira became a special class within Trinidadian society, the "Syrians." Immigrants from the United States were predominantly black. The British colonial government laid aside tracts of land near Princes Town for American slaves who fought against the United States in the War of 1812. Their so-called company villages remain, and their descendants have influenced religious practices on the island.[4]

Indentured laborers were imported from China and India between 1845 and 1917. Importation of Chinese labor was a limited success because many returned home after their period of indenture was completed. Indians, on the other hand, remained as wage laborers. Many bought land in Trinidad and settled permanently on the island. According to a recent census, Trinidad's population is roughly 45 percent East Indian and 45 percent black, with the remainder classified as white, colored (creole), Chinese, or Syrian. In 1976, East Indian political leaders claimed that the government census of 1960 had been falsified so as to underrepresent East Indians, who believe themselves to be the majority of the island population (see Table 1). At the time of this writing, figures from the 1970 census have yet to be released in their entirety.

Population growth has been sporadic. It slowed somewhat in the second half of this century, and between 1946 and 1960 the annual rate of growth was only 2.8 percent. Between 1960 and 1970 the rate of growth fell to less than 2.1 percent, a very low rate for the Caribbean. Preliminary analysis of the 1980 census shows a 13.7 percent increase over the 1970 population. While

Table 1
POPULATION OF TRINIDAD AND TOBAGO, 1960

Race	Male	Female	Total	Percentage
Negro	176,380	182,208	358,588	43.3
White	7,873	7,845	15,718	1.9
East Indian	153,043	148,903	301,946	36.5
Chinese	4,709	3,652	8,361	1.0
Mixed	65,178	69,571	134,749	16.3
Other	4,228	4,076	8,304	1.0
Not stated	169	122	291	0.0
Total	411,580	416,377	827,957	100.0

SOURCE: Central Statistical Office, Government of Trinidad and Tobago, *Population Census, 1960*, Vol. II, Part A.

not as dramatic as that of Barbados, the island has one of the highest population densities in the Americas.

Emigration, as on other West Indian islands, plays an important part in island life. Trinidadians are extremely mobile, and between 1972 and 1973 emigration brought about a population loss, from 1,148,000 to 1,061,850.[5] Individuals living abroad, especially in Canada and the United States, account for most of this loss. In addition, many Trinidadians visit relatives in the United States and Canada once or twice a year. An interesting aspect of Caribbean research is the large number of informants who are able to give directions to Spiritual Baptist and other religious centers, not only in Trinidad but in New York City and Hartford, Connecticut, as well. Caribbean peoples, possibly because they are so often at the periphery of world events, conceive themselves as "citizens of the world."

For most of Trinidad's history under British rule, it was a Crown Colony, with executive authority vested in governors appointed by the queen. The Constitution of 1950 did provide for a legislative body; however, truly representative government did not come to the island until 1956.[6] Complete independence from Great Britain was attained in 1962, and Trinidad and Tobago became a republic within the Commonwealth of Nations in 1976.

Since 1962, Trinidad has had a parliamentary system of government. Until his death in 1981, Eric Eustace Williams, a former professor of history at Howard University in Washington,

D.C., was prime minister. Williams's party remains in power under the leadership of George Chambers. At present, there are two major parties: the People's National Movement (PNM) under Chambers, and the Democratic Labour Party, representing the East Indian community.[7] There are several splinter groups as well, like the Workers' and Farmers' Party, the Butler Party, and Tapia. As population figures demonstrate, in order to win an election, parties must gain support within both the East Indian and black communities. In the 1976 election, the PNM was able to do this and won by a large majority. In the 1981 election, the PNM won twenty-six out of thirty-six seats. Critics complain that to do so, the PNM compromised on many issues vital to the black community.

Other matters of contention include the viability of Trinidad and Tobago as a unified nation-state. In 1888, the two islands (approximately twenty-one miles apart) were united by the British for administrative purposes and have remained a single political unit. Differences in wealth have led to talk of independence for Tobago, but the government in Port of Spain has not been receptive to demands for self-rule. Many fear the island of Tobago would not be able to "go it alone," and hope that desires for independence will eventually subside. Others predict that open conflict, such as that between St. Kitts and Anguilla in 1967, may break out between the islands. I find this doubtful.

Trinidad differs from its West Indian neighbors, including Tobago, in many ways. It is one of the wealthiest nations in the Caribbean, with abundant oil reserves, one of the largest oil refineries in the hemisphere, asphalt, sugar, and some large-scale manufacturing. In recent years, Trinidad has enjoyed a favorable balance of trade, and has frequently lent money to its underdeveloped neighbors both directly and through the World Bank. Also, unlike many Caribbean islands, Trinidad lacks a landed aristocracy equivalent to the Bekes of Martinique. Many creole planters lost their land in the nineteenth century, and today ownership is confined largely to members of the East Indian community, who have become Trinidad's landlords.

The world oil boom has resulted in a high rate of economic growth for the island. Individuals have been encouraged to buy on credit. Even poorer members of the society are issued department store charge accounts and the ever-present Barclay-card—many trips to the United States and Europe are financed by Barclay Bank. Prices are higher for clothing and manufactured goods, especially electronic equipment, than in the United States; but inflation is between 18 and 20 percent per year, and people recognize that things will cost more if they wait to buy. Between 1976 and 1978, my research expenses quadrupled. I was able to stay for three and a half months in 1976 for what it cost me for each month of research in 1978. Since my living arrangements were different in 1982, comparisons are not possible.

Inflation has widened the gap between rich and poor members of the society and has resulted in a new class of entrepreneurs. Those who have remained within the peasant economy and those on fixed incomes, such as old-age pensions or retirement benefits, have suffered greatly in the new economic order. To some extent the old (peasant) system was based on barter, while the new system deals exclusively in cash. Shopkeepers, especially in the countryside, used to take home-grown produce in exchange for manufactured items. This is no longer the case.

In many ways, Trinidad has become an advanced, industrialized nation. Its inhabitants enjoy a relatively high standard of living and participate in a competitive, capitalist economy where upward mobility is highly valued. Leaders in the Baptist faith claim that they are not a part of this competitive system. The focus of the Baptist religion, they say, is "not of this world." In this presentation, however, it will become apparent that Baptist leaders do compete and that they are much more interested in upward mobility than they are willing to acknowledge.

Economic mobility, while far from universal, is prevalent. Many formerly impoverished people have joined the ranks of the growing middle class. Spiritual Baptists, too, have become comparatively wealthy. Previous studies of Caribbean religions have dealt with black churches primarily in terms of poverty and deprivation.[8] In assessing some consequences of affluence for these religions, it will be demonstrated that many traits, once thought to be the direct result of poverty, persist in the face of newly acquired wealth and power.

It is no longer tenable to look at religion in the Caribbean as an avenue of redress for thwarted ambitions and deprivation.

If the purpose of these religions were to provide alternate systems of prestige, then the religions would decline as other mechanisms for obtaining prestige became available. This does not seem to have happened. In the case of Shango, economic and political advancement has meant, in many instances, that participants are able to sponsor more and better—more elaborate—feasts. In the case of the Spiritual Baptist church, it has meant larger church buildings and bigger church budgets.

Changes in ethnic and economic stratification (see Figure 2) have had an impact on religious affiliation. In the early 1900s, white Europeans occupied most dominant positions within the society, and the color of a person's skin was an important determinant of social status. It was common in this period for mulattos and/or "colored" to differentiate themselves from the black masses.[9] With the advent of "Black Power" in the 1960s, many of these same individuals who once separated themselves from any hint of "blackness" now brag of their "pure" African heritage. In this inversion of status, many institutions associated with traditional black culture have tended to benefit.[10]

Researchers have noted, however, that many religions have not benefited from the Black Power movement.[11] In Trinidad some groups, such as Shango, have grown, while Spiritual Baptists feel that their religion has remained stable. Baptist association with white Christianity may have vitiated its appeal among some members of the population. Also, Baptist leadership, at least in Curepe, tends to be politically conservative. Church elders opposed reform movements in the 1930s under T. Uriah Butler and more recently opposed the 1970 revolution. Leaders of other religious groups actively supported the attempted coup, while most Baptist leaders felt that the coup was an evil plot to bring communism to Trinidad. Many Baptist leaders also felt that they should support the government of Williams because, they believed, he was a fellow Baptist. Attempts to determine Williams's true status in the faith have not been successful. I did talk to a leader in Barataria, a town on the Eastern Main Road near Curepe, who claims to have baptized Williams in 1956;[12] however, other Baptists claim that this could not be true because Williams did not go to Barataria in 1956. Whatever the case, many Baptists do believe that the prime minister was a

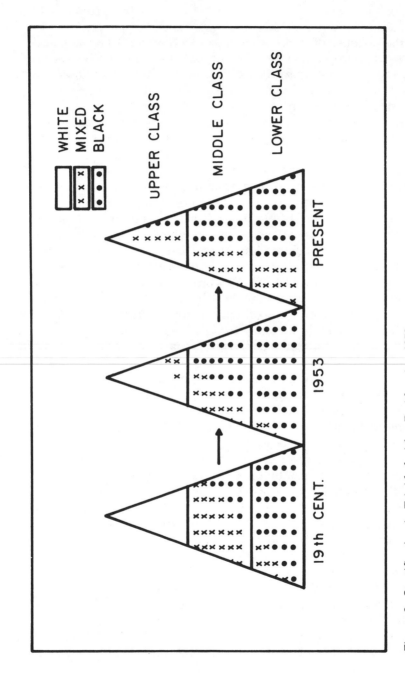

Figure 2. Stratification in Trinidad. After Braithwaite, 1953.

WHITE
MIXED
BLACK

UPPER CLASS
MIDDLE CLASS
LOWER CLASS

19th CENT.   1953   PRESENT

18

member of their faith, and he made no attempt to deny it. One consideration may be that Baptists provide support for progressive economic programs—programs that they would not support if they had not believed that Williams was a fellow Baptist.

In 1976, three Baptist leaders, from Fyzabad, Arima, and Tunapuna, respectively, ran for national office. They used their Baptist affiliations extensively in newspaper advertisements and in campaign literature, and each ran on a different party platform. Essentially, their programs could be classified as "conservative," but their priorities differed. All failed to be elected.

In their religions, as in other aspects of their lives, Trinidadians are pluralists. They may attend religious services at different churches on different days of the week and, on different occasions, may espouse contradictory opinions.

Cultural pluralism has long been seen as a dominant factor in Caribbean cultures. As Daniel Crowley noted for Trinidad, "A Trinidadian may be a Negro in appearance, a Spaniard in name, a Roman Catholic at church, an obeah practitioner in private, a Hindu at lunch, a Chinese at dinner, a Portuguese at work, and a Colored at the polls."[13]

While Crowley may have overstated his case, it is apparent that Trinidadian religious, political, and even kinship affiliations are not exclusivistic and that a person may assume many different roles and belief systems in the course of a lifetime. Selection of one political party or religious group need not preclude selection of another dissimilar group.

It must be noted, however, that individuals in plural societies often do find themselves under considerable pressure to adopt only one role as they mature, that is, to be either a Roman Catholic or a Hindu or an obeah practitioner. The assumption is sometimes made that pluralism results in greater freedom for all members of plural societies. This is not the case.

The Curepe Community

Curepe, where I lived while conducting research in 1976 and 1978, is a suburban residential community eight miles from Trinidad's capital, Port of Spain. It is located on the Eastern Main Road between the capital and Arima, the third-largest city on the island. From 1970 to 1980 the Curepe community grew from 11,106 to 12,072, a 9 percent increase.

Curepe is what American sociologists might term a "bedroom community," with a majority of its residents commuting daily to the capital. Limited employment opportunities exist in Curepe itself. There is some small-scale manufacturing and several stores, but most residents shop in neighboring St. Augustine, Tunapuna, or San Juan. Economic activity centers on a number of petty entrepreneurs who own "snackettes" and parlours, a small central market where fresh produce is available on Wednesdays and Sundays, and a small woolens mill that produces, among other things, sweaters for export.

Religious activities occupy a preponderant place in the community, as evidenced by the large number of churches. Within an area of twenty blocks there are a Catholic church, a Presbyterian church, an Episcopal (Anglican) church, a Seventh Day Adventist church, four nondenominational Christian groups ("Open Bible," etc.), several Hindu temples, a mosque, a large Pentecostal church, and, at last count, six Spiritual Baptist churches. The Pentecostal church, by far the largest and most influential religious body in the community, literally attracts worshippers from all over the island and throughout the Caribbean, Venezuela, and the Guianas.[14]

Between 1976 and 1982, the racial composition of the community has altered dramatically. Informants state that in 1970 nearly all Curepe residents were black; this has changed, and now most homes are occupied by East Indians. Harris Street, where I lived during 1976, was predominantly black; when I returned in 1978, only one black family remained. Rents in the area have increased, in some places quadrupled, and Curepe has become beyond the means of many lower middle-class persons. My own rent in the community increased from $70 to $290 (Trinidad-Tobago dollars; the exchange rate in 1978 was $2.42TT to $1US). Another tendency has been for absentee landlords, usually East Indian, to return and occupy their Curepe property themselves.

Petty entrepreneurs have adapted to serve a new clientele. Parlours, for example, have become oriental food shops in order to attract East Indian patrons. Religious leaders also have been forced to adapt to demographic changes in the area and to appeal to the rapidly growing East Indian community in their midst. Spiritual Baptists have adapted by introducing items from Hindu and Muslim worship into their services and, whenever possible, have encouraged East Indian Baptist leaders, primarily from the South of the island, to visit as guest speakers.

Displaced blacks have not abandoned the community, however, and many now live within commuting distance of Curepe. They continue to frequent their old churches, parlours, snackettes, and so on. Transportation is easily arranged throughout the island, with hourly bus service and twenty-four-hour jitneys or public taxis. With few exceptions, to be discussed in relation to pilgrimages, transportation in Trinidad is not a problem. Service to all points is both frequent and inexpensive.

2 • The Belief System

IN THIS chapter, I will try to represent something of the diversity of beliefs held by those who call themselves Baptists. Heterodoxy is apparent not only among Spiritual Baptist churches but within individual churches as well. For this reason, any statement as to what the Baptists believe must be qualified by the terms "many," "some," or "most." My data indicate that differences within the faith do not correlate with any particular region of the country, social class, or ethnic group. The belief system of any individual church person may be examined best in terms of the individual's own history in the faith (who "convicted" the individual to the faith, when and where the individual has mourned, and the like).

Heterodoxy may serve positive adaptive functions. Pelto and Pelto have decried the uniformist orientation of most anthropological researchers.[1] Citing Wallace,[2] they note that many social systems would not work as well if all participants shared a common knowledge of the system. Heterogeneity permits the rise of a system more complex than most or any of the participants in a system would be able to comprehend and heterogeneity liberates the participants from the heavy burden of learning and knowing one another's motivations and cognitions.

In the Baptist case, both of these functions are evident. Heterogeneity has allowed the emergence of a belief system more complex than any one participant in the religion could be expected to understand (and the church has members of many levels of education and competence), and it also has liberated participants from the burden of understanding one another's motivations and cognitions. Despite these advantages, Baptists struggle with problems of unity. The greatest unifying factors within the faith are the baptism and mourning rites that are discussed in the next chapter.

All Baptists, whether or not they have Shango connections, are polytheists. They believe in a universe populated by a great variety of spirit beings and say that relations with these spirit beings are often unpredictable. Some Baptists, especially those involved in Shango, attempt to manipulate the spirit world through the use of rituals and incantations, while many other Baptists fear all spirits and avoid relations with them.

Baptists conceive the spirit world as hierarchical and complex; and, in many ways, the spirit world replicates the organization of their church. Authority relations, for example, are considered to be important in the spirit world but, like authority relations in the Spiritual Baptist church, are not clearly defined. In addition, spirits are said to possess many human qualities and vices. They may on occasion be greedy or generous, lustful or abstinent, active or lazy. Their powers are limited, and even well-intentioned efforts to help human beings may go awry. While some spirits, especially those invoked during Shango rituals, are thought to possess humans, other spirits are said to fear men and to prefer remaining unnoticed.

By and large, spirits believed to possess human beings are more powerful than other, frequently unnamed, spirits. Essentially, the Baptists conceive a three-tier system wherein lesser spirits answer directly to Shango deities, and Shango deities answer directly to members of the Holy Trinity. In practice, however, many Baptists recognize that the spirits do not always follow this chain of command.

Lesser Spirits

For many Baptists, distinctions within the spirit world are unimportant. These believers lump all spirits, with the exception of members of the Holy Trinity, together and label them as "orisha" or "jumbies." This usage is not common to other West Indian islands, such as Montserrat, where the term "orisha" refers exclusively to "African" gods, and the term "jumbie" is reserved for spirits of the dead.[3] Among my informants, however, the terms were used interchangeably.

Baptists who participate in Shango ceremonies make a distinction between spirits that have been incarnate and spirits that have never been incarnate. The former are said to be more powerful than the latter. Both African gods (Shango, Oshun, et al.) and Catholic saints are said to have been incarnate, a major difference being that African gods once lived in Africa while Catholic saints once lived in Europe. African gods and Catholic saints are accorded equal status, but contrary to the statements of Herskovits and Simpson,[4] they are never confused. Differences in personality and power are noted frequently, and one would never ask of St. Peter what would best be accomplished by Oshun or Shankpara.[5]

For Baptists who practice Shango rituals, saints and African gods may serve as intermediaries between devotees and other members of the spirit world. Because certain spirits are said to have been incarnate, these spirits are believed to understand human needs and desires better. Although they are said to understand human beings, they cannot be expected to be sympathetic to all human requests. At best these spirits are approachable, while at worst they may be unpredictable and ineffectual.

Shangoists, Baptists, and other Trinidadians believe in another category of spirit beings who are said to take human form but are never believed to have been incarnate. These spirits occupy an anomalous position halfway between man and beast. Among these are several spirits adopted from European folk tradition called jables, lagahus, and sukoiyaas; respectively, succubi, werewolves, and vampires.[6]

Jables deal most directly with men. They may take the form of beautiful women and attempt to seduce men in their dreams. It is said that if a man succumbs to temptation, he will be the jables' slave in the next world. Spiritual Baptists believe that nocturnal emissions are caused by jables and prescribe potions in order to keep them away. Many Baptist men sleep with Bibles under their pillows to ward off jables and to keep their minds from "wandering to the flesh" in their dreams.

Lagahus, or werewolves, are said to roam the night but are not thought to be particularly dangerous to Baptists.[7] Sukoiyaas, or vampires, on the other hand, are believed to warrant greater concern. Lagahu attacks are infrequent; however, sukoiyaa attacks are believed to be common among Baptists. Cases of hookworm, leukemia, and anemia are often attributed to sukoiyaas, who are said to develop a taste for an individual's blood and return nightly until the victim is "dry."

Potions and a Bible under the pillow are said to be relatively effective against sukoiyaas; however, some Baptists do fall victim to attack. Members of the faith are reluctant to seek medical treatment for blood ailments, since this would imply inadequate defenses against the sukoiyaas. One of my informants, dying of leukemia, claims publicly that she has "fatal diabetes." Her daughter, who knows of her condition, has tried to get her to accept a blood transfusion and chemotherapy—thus far without success. In this case, as in other cases, Baptist notions of etiology may preclude outside medical treatment.

Spirit beings are also said to be found in association with land, trees, rocks, and bodies of water. Every piece of land, for example, has its own spirit inhabitants, and any disturbance of the land— such as construction of a house or a church—is likely to meet with spiritual resistance. Baptist rites of purification, to be described elsewhere, are seen as one effective means of combating these spirits. People of many faiths hire Spiritual Baptists for this purpose. Other religious practitioners, such as obeahmen and Catholic priests, also are willing to provide such services, but at greater cost. Leader R. claimed to have performed purification rites at the sites of the Catholic, Pentecostal, and Seventh Day Adventist churches in Curepe. The rites did not receive official sanction from the religious bodies involved but were necessary before workmen were willing to begin construction.

The Trinity

However little some Baptists distinguish among members of the spirit world, all Baptists distinguish between orisha and/or jumbies and members of the Holy Trinity. Members of the Trinity are the highest of all spirits. Both the world of men and the world of the spirits are under their control.

Within the Trinity, there is no clearly developed notion of

unity. God the Father, God the Son, and God the Holy Ghost are understood to be three separate entities.[8] Each member of the Trinity is said to carry on his activities independent of the other members. God the Son, for example, is often unaware of the activities of God the Father, and vice versa. In ceremonies, it is seen as essential that each ritual be repeated three times if the attention of all three members of the Trinity is desired.

Prayer and supplication may be directed to only one member of the Trinity at a time. Particular requests are directed to different members; for example, God the Son is believed to be most sympathetic to human needs because he at one time took human form. The Holy Ghost, on the other hand, is seen as more effective in dealing with problems in the spirit world, while God the Father, as creator of the earth, is called upon in times of flood, hurricanes, and other natural disasters.

Some problems do not fall clearly within the domain of any one member of the Trinity. To remedy this, several prayers may be offered. This is especially true when addressing God the Father. There is hierarchical ranking within the Trinity, with God the Father occupying the highest position. While it is possible to address God the Father directly, it is believed to be more effective to address God the Father indirectly through God the Son or God the Holy Ghost. Multiple prayers assure that "the message gets through."

Various potions (communion wine, holy water, etc.) and ritual objects have power by association with individual members of the Trinity. Holy water, for example, is associated predominantly with the Holy Ghost; communion wine with God the Son; and the Bible is associated strongly with God the Father.

The Bible is especially valued for the power and wisdom contained therein. It is considered desirable among members of the faith to have many Bibles in many languages. Prominent leaders (and those who would be prominent) possess extensive Bible collections including, whenever possible, volumes in Greek and Hebrew. These are said to be useful in divining ("proving") and curing. None of my informants has any knowledge of Greek or Hebrew; in fact, several older informants, including one with over fifty Bibles in his collection, are unable to read. Illiterate

Baptists attempt to disguise their inability to read by committing long passages of the King James version to memory.

Baptists take the Bible seriously as the "Word of God" or more specifically, the word of God the Father; however, since God the Father is so far removed from human affairs, his word is often inscrutable. Bible passages must be read and reread many times before the true meaning becomes apparent. Even after many hours of careful scrutiny, the meaning of a verse may remain obscure, and Baptists must call upon the Holy Ghost for assistance in interpreting the text.

Communion wine has power as an extension of God the Son; however, it is not widely used in ritual contexts—as it is used in the Roman Catholic tradition—because it has negative connotations. Communion rites are seldom performed in the Spiritual Baptist tradition, once or twice a year, and the rites are poorly attended.[9] One Baptist told me he did not like to attend communion because it made him feel like a sukoiyaa or vampire "sucking the blood of Christ." Another informant said that communion was cannibalistic because "you eats the body and blood of Jesus."

Members of the faith are also uneasy concerning Christ's sacrifice on the cross. While some Baptists may perform animal sacrifices, all Baptists believe that human sacrifice is wrong and have great difficulty accepting it in the case of Jesus on the cross. According to Baptist belief, when Christ died on the cross he was a human being. How, then, did God the Father permit this abomination to occur?

The crucifix, probably the most prominent symbol in the orthodox Christian tradition, is also played down because of its association with human sacrifice. Believers do recognize the power of the crucifix but choose not to display crucifixes in their homes or to wear them on their persons. A small crucifix is displayed, however, on the top of the altar of each church.

The ritual most commonly associated with God the Son is anointment with oil. Anointment takes place both before and after baptismal rites and the mourning ceremony, and it is also very important in healing. Leaders readily admit that anointment is not as powerful as communion wine or the crucifix, but since there are negative connotations associated with the latter, various other symbols are substituted in their places.

A variety of ritual paraphernalia is associated with members of the Holy Trinity, but correspondence is incomplete. Many ritual items have no correspondences at all; however, given the intensely pluralistic setting, the number of condensed symbols is much greater than anticipated. Bells rung both before and during worship represent God the Father. When a bell rings, I was told, it is the "voice of God." Candles, when lighted, represent the Holy Ghost; and flowers—because Christ spent time in the Garden of Gethsemane—represent God the Son. Chromolithographs of Jesus, never on the cross; the saints; and, in some cases, the Virgin Mary represent their respective deities. However, chromolithographs are not said to have any power in themselves. In several Curepe churches, Vishnu, Krishna, and other Hindu deities are posted either in the back of the church or on the left wall of the church. These, too, are not believed to have any special power.

Other Beliefs

Separation of powers and focus within the Trinity is paralleled by a separation of powers and focus within the individual. Baptist ethnopsychology recognizes three distinct aspects of personhood: mind, body, and spirit. Each aspect of personhood corresponds roughly to a member of the Trinity. Body, because it is incarnate, is associated with God the Son; mind, because it is creative, is associated with God the Father; and spirit, because it cannot be seen, touched, or smelled, is associated with God the Holy Ghost.

All aspects of personhood are considered positive, although many Baptists believe that the body and spirit should be subordinate to the mind. Wisdom and creative power are considered the highest goods in the Baptist faith, and those who seek after wisdom are accorded high prestige within the religion.

Baptists claim that their rituals devote attention to the entire person. The body is trained by "exercise" and deprivation, the spirit is trained by song and prayer, and the mind is trained by visions and dreams. Dreams, in this case, are believed to have an existence outside the individual and to provide knowledge that transcends waking experience.[10]

The purpose of ritual, according to Baptist informants, is simply to enhance one's opportunities to obtain "high-quality" dreams and visions. Rituals provide a setting conducive to dreaming, but the proper setting is not seen as a necessity. Theoretically, visions obtained outside the mourning room should also be accorded special status. What is stated in theory, however, is not always followed closely in practice. Baptist leaders are much more likely to question visions received without benefit of ceremony, and many leaders are wary of independent visions. Most leaders suggest that members should participate in a ceremony to confirm visions received independently. On an individual level, all dreams and visions are "true," while at the institutional level, those visions obtained in a specific ritual context are believed to be "more true" than all other dreams and visions.

Many dreams, even those obtained in a proper ritual context, do not come true. In order for a dream to be fulfilled, it is said that all aspects of an individual's personhood—body, mind, and spirit—must "pull together," and such consensus is rare. Dreams (from God the Father), for example, may be incompatible with the body or the spirit. When consensus is lacking, even valid dreams are not realized.

Baptists recognize that some dreams are not sent by God the Father. Orisha may use visions and dreams to manipulate humans, often with much success. Moreover, dreams can give an individual power to do evil in the world. Obeahmen, for example, derive much of their power from visions and dreams. It is very important, according to many Baptists, that dreams be used only for positive ends.

Ethical concerns are important to some Spiritual Baptists. Leaders admonish their followers not to steal, drink rum to excess, or swear in public. A number of followers take these admonitions seriously. Other followers state that "the gods, they don' care how we acts." Leaders, for the most part, regret that they do not have more control over their followers, and continue to make ethical pronouncements whenever they deem it to be appropriate.

A majority of Baptists in my sample are very much concerned

with maintaining proper family relations. A man, it is said, should live with one woman only. It appears to make little difference whether a man and woman are legally married, that is, married in the eyes of the government or in the eyes of the church. On the other hand, most Baptists in my Curepe sample are legally married.

When compared to the Spiritual Baptists of St. Vincent, Trinidad's Baptists do not seem to be very much concerned with the afterlife. On St. Vincent and some other West Indian islands, Baptists sponsor elaborate wakes on the third, ninth, and fourteenth nights, and the sixth and twelfth months after a death.[11] Trinidadian Baptists do not sponsor multiple wakes for their members, nor do they feel that multiple wakes are necessary for non-Baptists. Rituals, according to my informants, cannot influence safe passage into Heaven.

Multiple wakes are held in the north-central region of Trinidad, where there has been considerable migration from Spanish and French islands of the Caribbean. Some Spiritual Baptist leaders, in fact, are quite willing to officiate at these wakes and claim that wakes are good for the family, even if wakes cannot help the deceased. Further, performance of wakes is seen as a good source of income (leaders charge between $8 and $10TT, $4 to $6US).

Baptists do not believe that a person's soul remains on earth for a period of time after death. All three aspects of personhood (mind, body, and spirit) ascend immediately into Heaven. This process is seen as automatic, and there is nothing humans can do to change it. When asked about Heaven, many Baptists confessed that they knew little about it. Several informants told me that Heaven is very much like here (earth) "only better." Other informants asserted, with equal conviction, that life in Heaven is very much different from life on earth; a major difference is that people do not have bodies in Heaven. A large number of informants, when asked to provide details on the afterlife, replied that they had not given the matter much thought. I do not believe that they were being evasive on this point. The afterlife does not seem to be a central focus of the religion.

While belief in Heaven does play a small part in the Spiritual Baptist belief system, belief in Hell is not at all prevalent.[12] Many

Baptists flatly refuse to entertain the notion that there could be such as place as Hell. Those Baptists who do entertain notions of Hell are former members of other religious denominations, such as the Methodists, Pentecostals, or London Baptists. Several members claim that Hell does exist for Pentecostals, Methodists, and London Baptists—but that now that they are Spiritual Baptists they do not have to worry about Hell.

The Baptist faith is a religion for the here-and-now. Believers expect to derive concrete benefits from their associations with the church. If a man attends worship regularly, participates in mourning rites occasionally, and gives money toward the work of the church, he and his family should prosper and be healthy. When problems arise in the life of the individual, it is said to be because the individual has not kept his or her obligations in the faith.

Baptist notions of the Trinity, their de-emphasis of the crucifixion, their belief in the Bible as a magical book that has efficacy in and of itself, their overly literal interpretation of the scriptures, and their lack of interest in the afterlife call into question the extent to which the religion may be understood as a part of the Christian tradition. Baptists consider themselves as a part of this tradition, but some scholars have expressed reservations. Herskovits and Herskovits, for example, treated the faith as an independent cult, and played down Christian influences, even though the Toco groups studied evidenced few African retentions and many Christian elements.[13] Henney, on the other hand, placed Vincentian Baptists squarely and unequivocally within the Christian tradition.[14]

Participants and nonparticipants in Shango alike emphatically state that the Baptists should be included within Christianity but as a separate denomination, like the Presbyterians, the London Baptists, the Adventists, or the Pentecostals. They also state that Baptists are part of a unified church and not, as others have claimed, fragmented cults or sects. Admittedly, most Baptist leaders do not know the difference between churches, sects, and cults—at least not as these categories of organization are understood in the sociology of religion—but several leaders have read scholarly accounts of their religion and insist that "whatever a cult is, we is not one."

I support their protestations with reservations. Baptist forms of church organization and denominational hierarchies are loose when compared to those of Catholicism or Presbyterianism but are no less structured than the organization of many Pentecostal groups. Baptist attitudes toward their faith are pragmatic, but they are no less oriented toward the here-and-now than many other "Christian" religious groups on the islands; and if an overly literal interpretation of selected passages of the Bible were grounds for exclusion from the Christian tradition, many Fundamentalist groups would have been excluded long ago.

I believe that differences of interpretations among Henney, Herskovits and Herskovits, and Simpson may reveal as much about Western biases in the study of non-Western Christianity as they do of the religion itself. The Baptists are extremely conservative in some aspects of their faith. They are both flexible and rigid; heterodox and orthodox. Even their most exotic ritual, the mourning ceremony, is not without Biblical justification (Daniel 10), and they are quick to point out other Biblical precedents, such as when "Christ himself 'mourned' in the wilderness for forty days."

The problem may be that many Western scholars associate religious conservatism (as found in some aspects of the Spiritual Baptist faith) with orthodoxy, whereas many Caribbean religions manage to be both conservative and heterodox at the same time.[15] The Spiritual Baptists have just such a religion.

Origin Myths

Origins of the Spiritual Baptist church in Trinidad are not clear. In discussing the matter with Baptist leaders, three distinct origin myths emerge. Some leaders, mainly those who sponsor Shango ceremonies, contend that the faith is an outgrowth of various forms of African religious traditions prevalent in urban areas of Trinidad during the late nineteenth century, while others, mainly Vincentians and their descendants, claim that the religion had its origins on St. Vincent and was brought to Trinidad in the early part of this century. Yet another origin myth credits the so-called 'Meriken Baptists with bringing the faith to the island. Each origin myth is supported by members of different factions within the church, and significantly, no respondents argued for a Trinidad provenience. All claimed that the faith began elsewhere and was brought to Trinidad. In the first case, Baptists stress their legitimacy by emphasizing "African" roots, while in the latter two myths, Baptists stress their legitimacy by emphasizing Methodist and Baptist roots, respectively.

Proponents of the first myth state that Trinidad has one of the oldest and "purest" traditions of African religion in the New World—sometimes citing Herskovits or Andrew Carr to that effect. Historical data support their contention that some aspects of Trinidadian religion are directly from Africa. Following emancipation in the British West Indies, free Africans were encouraged to immigrate to Trinidad to expand agricultural production there. Between 1841 and 1861, Trinidad received 6,581 free Africans representing a number of cultural groupings including Ibo, Temme, Wolof, Yoruba, Ashanti, Fulani, and Mandingo peoples.[16]

These new peoples, of course, brought many of their religious beliefs with them to the New World, and among the migrants were two *vodunsi* (initiates) and a Dahomean *hubono* (high priest). The *hubono*, Robert Antoine, established a Rada compound in the Belmont neighborhood of Port of Spain. He was able to maintain a substantial portion of the Dahomean ceremonial calendar, and his compound became a center for migrant Dahomeans in Trinidad.[17] Services at the Rada compound, it is contended, inspired many other forms of African worship on the island including those forms later known as Shango and the Spiritual Baptists.

It is unclear exactly what influence the Rada community had on other forms of African ceremonies in Trinidad. The religion itself was short lived. After Antoine's death in 1899, his followers ceased to maintain the Dahomean ceremonial calendar, and no new *vodunsi* have yet appeared to continue this tradition. The center continues to operate in Belmont, but in a greatly altered form. It is currently dominated by two women who make their livings primarily by giving consultations and casting *obi* (divining).

In many respects, the Dahomean religion is very different from that of the Shango religion in Trinidad. Carr claims that in the Shango tradition devotees may be possessed by many gods, while in the Dahomean tradition a god selects one person to be his devotee for life. When that person dies, the god may select another person to be his devotee or, as seems to have happened in Belmont, refuse to manifest until someone is found who is "worthy" to receive him. Thus, a god may disappear from ceremonial ritual for several generations if a worthy successor to his devotee is not found.

Shango services are much more flexible. There are no fixed relations between individual devotees and members of the pantheon. Different individuals may be possessed by the same god within a single religious ceremony; moreover, two or more individuals may claim to be possessed by the same god simultaneously. A major function of Shango leaders is to determine which individual is truly possessed by Oshun or Shankpara and which individual is possessed by a lesser spirit "pretending" to be Oshun or Shankpara.

Differences between Shango ritual and that of Rada constitute only one possible objection to this origin myth. Even if the transition from Rada to Shango were clear, the transition from Rada to the Baptist faith is problematic. Some Shangoists claim that Baptist ceremonies once served as a "cover" for African practices. In order to avoid government persecution, Shango leaders called their religious centers Baptist "churches." The problem, however, is that there is no evidence that Spiritual Baptist churches were better accepted by the authorities than forms of African worship. The decision to adopt Baptist ritual as a "cover" would not seem to have been a very good or logical choice.

Neither Shango nor the Spiritual Baptists occupied a position of "respectability" within their society, and it would have been difficult for Shangoists to use the Baptist name to give their religion additional prestige. Norman Paul, himself a devotee of Oshun, stated, "I was told not to allow any Baptists to have dealings with me, because according to what I know they lives an immoral life. When they goes to mourn the people the leaders have dealings with them as husband and wife . . . they make all kinds of things to hurt people using this same book (the Sixth and Seventh Books of Moses), and that is how the people who make obeah and so on does."[18] I encountered many of these same fears in conversations with non-Baptists during 1976. Such feelings are prevalent not only among the poor and uneducated but the educated as well. Friends at the University of the West Indies (St. Augustine) warned me that it was too dangerous to study the Baptists because they practice witchcraft.

In my first year of field research, a Baptist leader customarily waited for me on the front stairs of my rooming house. The next year, my landlady, a well-educated East Indian, suggested that my stay would be too short to allow me to rent a room at her house and that I might want to live at the university. It was only in 1978, after the Baptist leader in question had died, that my landlady admitted that she was afraid the Baptist would work obeah on her, or, more important, on her animals and crops. She was a Pentecostal and felt that while her religion would protect her, it would not protect her animals and crops because she could not bring them to church with her.

Baptist leaders, aware that people fear them, sometimes attempt to turn this to their advantage. Whenever Leader D. has trouble hailing a jitney on a busy evening, he steps into the middle of the road, forcing the vehicle to stop for him. He claims that jitneys do not like to pick up Baptists (in these cases he is immediately identifiable as a Baptist because he is carrying a shepherd's crook and other ritual implements), but no driver would be willing to risk hitting a Baptist. "They fears our obeah," he added.

Baptists are often resentful that their church is not considered to be "respectable" within the larger community. They go to great lengths in order to appear "like the other religions" (London Baptists, Presbyterians, Methodists, etc.) and would very much like to be accepted. Baptist leaders make a point of attending ecumenical services on the island, whether or not invited, and whenever possible invite other denominational ministers to attend their services.

Those who claim that the religion originated in St. Vincent point out that the central ritual of the faith, the mourning ceremony, began there. They recognize that similar ceremonies exist on other islands and in other religions, but "no other people calls it 'mourning' nor does they understands its true Biblical significance." Parallel ceremonies are noted in Christian, African, and Amerindian traditions, but the Spiritual Baptists say that only they know the "true" practice. Catholic priests, I was told, engage in a ritual similar to mourning. "They goes on what they calls 'retreats' and does just what Baptists does."[19] Africans, it is said, mourn, too, but for different reasons.

According to Henney, Spiritual Baptists in St. Vincent insist that John and Charles Wesley were the founders of their religion.[20] The Methodist movement, begun by John Wesley, was dedicated to the attempt to "recapture life according to the precepts of the Primitive Church through fasting, prayer, meditating, and searching to know the Divine Will."[21] The religion reached the West Indies in 1790, when Nathaniel Gilbert, the speaker in the House of Assembly in Antigua, began preaching the gospel to slaves. From Antigua, it reached St. Vincent, where it is reported to have been well received.[22]

In 1792, laws were passed aimed at discouraging Methodist missionary activity on the island, and converts were left to develop their own religion. The present-day Spiritual Baptist church is said to stem from the religious beliefs and practices of those early converts.

Throughout the early decades of this century, migration was a constant factor in West Indian social life, especially migration from the poorer islands such as St. Vincent and Grenada to Trinidad. Twenty-two of my Baptist informants migrated from St. Vincent between 1913 and 1928, and most claim to have migrated for "economic reasons."

This period of rapid migration corresponds roughly to a period of growth for Trinidad's Spiritual Baptist churches. Migration, however, cannot fully account for the religion's apparent success on the island. Vincentians, and it may be surmised Vincentian Baptists, migrated to other islands where the Spiritual Baptist faith never developed, for example, St. Kitts, Nevis, Barbados, St. Lucia, Curacao, and Aruba. Why, then, did the Spiritual Baptist church flourish in Trinidad and not in some of these other locations? The Spiritual Baptists may have originated in St. Vincent, but the religion must have met with favorable conditions in Trinidad in order to persist.

Those who claim that the Spiritual Baptists in Trinidad are an outgrowth of the 'Meriken Baptist church contend that the 'Meriken Baptists provided just such a favorable environment. Underhill credits an Englishman, George Cowen, with establishing the first Baptist missionary outpost in Trinidad;[23] however, Stewart asserts that the Baptist faith was introduced thirty years earlier by American black refugees who had fought on the side of the British in the War of 1812.[24] Between May 1815 and August 1816, 781 black Baptists from South Carolina settled in Trinidad. More than 70 percent settled in the south-central section of Naparima on Crown lands. There was considerable resistance to the American settlers in Naparima, and many were forced to relocate in so-called company villages—named after the companies to which the former British marines had belonged: First, Second, Third, and so forth. Religious services held in the company villages included behavior recorded as "Shouting."[25]

Many differences are noted between religious practices of the 'Meriken Baptists and those of present-day Spiritual Baptists. There was, as mentioned previously, no mourning ceremony among the 'Meriken Baptists, and, in addition, the 'Meriken Baptists do not seem to have practiced glossolalia.[26] Trinidadian Baptists who support American origins of their religion often do so as a means of protesting what they see as Vincentian domination of their faith. Many powerful leaders in Trinidad are Vincentians, and it is felt that these leaders favor the advancement of fellow Vincentians within church hierarchies, sometimes excluding native-born Trinidadians from positions of authority. Also, there are very strong pro-American feelings in some sections of Trinidad. Many seek to establish connections between themselves and blacks in the United States. The 'Meriken Baptists are seen as part of a very noble tradition of black resistance. They are said to have fought against their masters, sided with the British, and gained their freedom; this is not exactly the case.[27] The most important consideration, I believe, is that 'Meriken Baptists and their descendants no longer exert direct influence in the religion. Vincentians, on the other hand, appear as a real and ever-present influence.

Nineteenth-century 'Meriken Baptists and twentieth-century Spiritual Baptists seem to have shared a belief in the efficacy of dreams for predicting the future and for revealing otherwise unseen qualities in potential leaders of the faith. Methods of choosing a pastor among the 'Meriken Baptists were similar to those used by the Spiritual Baptists of today: "When a pastor was to be chosen, meetings were held nightly during which potential candidates were given the opportunity to 'set the church to pray.' Simultaneously, members of the congregation submitted their dreams for or against the candidate to the elders. On the basis of the interpretation of submitted dreams, and the performances of the candidates, one was determined to have been 'called by the Lord' and was in turn called by the congregation."[28] In both groups, however, it is noted that dreams per se do not determine the selection of candidates. The most significant factor in each case is the way in which these dreams are interpreted by church leaders. This theme will be taken up again in our discussion of the Spiritual Baptist mourning ceremony.

The value of all three origin myths—African, Methodist, Baptist—is that they reveal something of the factionalism in the church. By adhering to one myth or another, an individual indicates his or her own background and experiences within the faith. Subscribing to one myth or another is, in short, a political statement.

I do not believe that it will ever be possible to trace the "true" origins of the Spiritual Baptist faith in Trinidad. There are connections between the Spiritual Baptists and African tribal religions, the Spiritual Baptists and Methodism on St. Vincent, and the Spiritual Baptists and the 'Meriken Baptists. Unfortunately, these connections are neither clear enough nor direct enough to make Baptist origins amenable to scientific inquiry.

Many Trinidadians confuse Spiritual Baptist ceremonies with those of Shango. Much of this confusion stems from a lack of exposure to Baptist ritual. Since Shango rites are conducted in open-air *palais*, their ceremonies are easily viewed, however briefly, by members of the community (see Appendix). Baptist rites, on the other hand, are conducted inside a building, and fewer Trinidadians take the trouble to find out what goes on during Baptist services. Although there are many differences between Baptist rites and those of Shango, many assume that these two ritual forms are similar.

A large number of Spiritual Baptists condemn Shango activities. They do not participate in Shango rites and oppose what they perceive as "African" elements within the Baptist faith. Several Baptists have gone to the extreme of picketing a Shango palais—usually on the afternoon prior to a Shango ceremony. Shango-Baptist relations will be discussed further in Chapter 4.

3 ● *Ritual*

Regular Services

REGULAR Spiritual Baptist religious ceremonies last from three to six hours. Services are held on Sundays, and in many churches services are held on Wednesday evenings as well. Leaders occasionally organize a series of special nightly worship services known as a "rally." Rallies may occur over a period of several weeks and do not differ markedly in form from regular worship.

Behavior during ceremonies varies considerably among churches. Most leaders begin their services with elaborate rites of purification, although this is not always the case. Some leaders—especially those who have served the same church for many years—believe that purification rites are unnecessary and may skip many steps in the ritual to be described below.

Purification rites are intended to cast out evil spirits—jumbies and orisha—from the place of worship. Candles, located at all church openings, are thought to discourage evil spirits from entering the church building while ceremonies are in progress; and incense, bell ringing, and "strewing" of perfumed water serve to dispel those spirits already inside. Unbaptized worshippers and visitors are believed to be most vulnerable to attack by evil spirits and receive special attention. There are also regional differences in the intensity of purification rites. Baptist leaders in Curepe, where a neighboring Pentecostal church specializes in demon exorcism,[1] take special care in purification rites because it is contended that an abundance of recently exorcised spirits are looking for new hosts in the area.

Rites of purification usually begin about one hour before the stated time of worship but are seldom completed before worship has begun. Between the start of worship and the completion of purification rites, the congregation sings slow, unemotional hymns said to keep the Holy Ghost from manifesting Himself before the building is "clean." As these slow hymns are being sung, a "surveyor" (who may be of either sex but is most often female) performs rituals to "fortify the church." The surveyor begins by curtsying at the center pole, picking up one of the bells and ringing it repeatedly. After curtsying again, a container of flowers and water is picked up, and the surveyor goes in turn to the east, west, north, and south corners of the church. Here he or she faces the wall, pours water on the floor, and curtsies. Later, he or she performs the same ritual at the altar (males approach the altar, females sprinkle water from a distance), in all the doorways, and at the center pole. These same motions are repeated throughout the service—sometimes with a bell, sometimes with a candle.

High-ranking church members sometimes do not appear until the service is well under way. In general, higher-ranking members should be among the last to arrive, and members who enter after high-ranking members are perceived to be challenging the authority of their superiors. Lower-ranking members, therefore, take special pains to arrive on time.

When the highest-ranking church member, also known as the "paramount leader," takes his place behind the altar, the service officially begins. From the altar, paramount leaders direct their followers in worship. They tell lower-ranking members when to read or recite (often from memory) Biblical passages and tell higher-ranking males when to provide enlightenment and interpretation of the scriptures. Men are invited to speak from the front of the church, while women must address the congregation kneeling at the center post. Women are never allowed behind the altar except to dust and mop.

Herskovits conceived Baptist ceremonies as a gradual progression from decorous "European" forms to so-called African forms: "The change from Baptist ritual to African-like 'shout' during a given service is gradual, for as it is often the case in

Africa itself, even the leader does not know when the spirit will come and possession will occur. Restraint, in the European sense, may reign for an hour or two after the beginning of a Sunday night ceremony, as actually was the case in at least several services visited. But sooner or later the restraint is broken."[2] In my experience, however, Baptist ceremonies tend to shift from quiet contemplation to frenzy and back again. The Baptists themselves refer to these as "cool" and "hot" periods. Specific types of behavior, such as glossolalia, are considered appropriate only during certain parts of the service. At other times, these same behaviors are deemed inappropriate. There is no gradual progression from one form of worship to another.

Baptists believe that the "hot" part of service should not begin until the paramount leader is firmly in control of the ceremonies. All spirits are thought to be potentially dangerous, and only a paramount leader is believed to be powerful enough to deal with them. Among Spiritual Baptists who perform Shango rites, intensification is a focal point of service and lasts from one to three hours. This, members claim, is to decrease the chance of Shango spirits manifesting during Baptist ceremonies, and in churches without Shango rites these rituals are considerably shorter.

Earlier researchers devoted much of their attention to "hot" aspects of service, sometimes to the exclusion of "cool" contemplative portions of worship. In terms of actual time (based on the analysis of over forty hours of service recorded between 1976 and 1982), Baptist services are over 70 percent "cool." This reflects the ascendancy of God the Father, who is associated with "cool" parts of the service. Wisdom, associated with contemplation and quiet, is considered the highest virtue within the faith.

During the "hot" parts of service, deliberate attempts are made to induce manifestations of the Holy Ghost. Various techniques are used, including hymn singing, hand clapping, and "adoption" (a form of hyperventilation). The combination of these techniques is known as "shouting" or "trumpeting in the Spirit."

"Shouting" takes a wide variety of forms. A grunt, a whisper, or a sigh may be interpreted as a manifestation of the Holy Ghost, while ten minutes of barks and nonsense syllables may

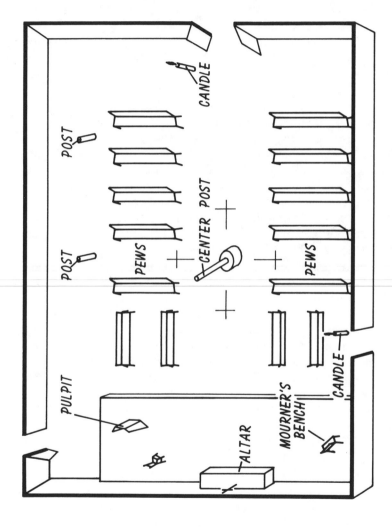

Figure 3. Floor Plan, Little Flock Spiritual Baptist Church, Curepe

44

not be so interpreted. As in other church affairs, paramount leaders decide whether an incident was truly a manifestation of the Holy Ghost or the individual was faking. Such decisions are usually made *a posteriori*.

I have identified three distinct types of verbalizations that are usually interpreted as manifestations of the Holy Ghost: (1) animal noises, especially noises similar to those made by chickens and dogs, (2) grunts and groans, and (3) "speech," either in the form of ordinary language or gibberish ("the unknown tongue"). All three forms are considered to be equally inspired.[3]

In most cases, those who are said to be possessed by the Holy Ghost jump up and down, gesticulate wildly, and speak loudly. Often at the conclusion of such an outburst, the possessed will collapse, to be retrieved by a member of the congregation or the paramount leader.

Amidst all this activity, lively hymns are sung. Music is central to this part of church ritual. Baptists use music to dispel unwanted spirits, to demonstrate power and authority within the church, to "guide" candidates for baptism and mourning, to offer prayer and supplication, and to invoke the presence of the Holy Ghost. Such uses of music are prevalent in both African[4] and Afro-American religious groups.

At this point in the service, hymns provide a very important means of demonstrating one's authority within the church. In some parts of the service, hymns follow a set pattern. This is especially true in the mourning ceremony, where songs complement whatever activity is occurring and act to create the proper frame of mind for the candidate.[5] It is less true, however, at regular services, where hymns are "weapons" in a battle for power.

During "hot" parts of regular services, any high-ranking member may attempt to lead the congregation in a particular hymn. Often, two or more members will attempt to lead different hymns simultaneously. Whichever hymn predominates is said to be the "will of God the Holy Ghost"; thus, the leader of that hymn is thought to be closer to God. There are churches on the island where such "battles of the spirit" are not encouraged. In such churches, paramount leaders choose all hymns, and the congregation simply follows his lead; even in these churches, dissident members will sometimes attempt to make the congregation stray from the paramount leader's choice.

Manifestations of the Holy Ghost are followed almost immediately by periods of illumination and contemplation. This part of the service, consisting of additional scripture readings and short homilies by various members of the congregation, is devoted to the Word of God. During periods of illumination, Biblical passages from the New Testament, especially the Gospel of John and the Book of Revelations, and the Books of Daniel, Psalms, and Ezekiel from the Old Testament are favored.

Homilies provide several, often contradictory, interpretations of each Biblical passage. Successive speakers point out fallacies in one another's interpretations and pray for greater enlightenment. Women also participate in this part of the service, but their interpretations of scripture are never acknowledged directly. Women voice their opinions in the form of a prayer.[6] While women's opinions are reiterated from time to time during debate, men do not credit women with a capacity for inspiration and often treat women's contributions as if they were their own inventions. In a discussion of the meaning of Daniel 4 ("the tree of great height at the center of the world"), Mother R. proposed that the church should replace metal poles with wooden poles so as to be more like "the tree of great height." Her suggestion was ignored for about twenty minutes until a man again brought up the issue of wooden poles for the church. After much serious deliberation, it was decided that wooden poles should be purchased—but at no time during deliberation was Mother R. acknowledged as one of the instigators of this idea.

All high-ranking churchmen and those who would aspire to high rank are expected to offer some illumination. This is one way to make one's talents known to the paramount leader, and it may also increase one's reputation within the church. Baptist etiquette dictates that all higher-ranking members should allow lower-ranking members to speak before them. This is very advantageous to high-ranking members who have longer to prepare their interpretations and may benefit from earlier discussion. Paramount leaders, in all cases, are the last to speak.

As each speaker concludes his interpretation, he begins a ritual of sharing and touching with other members of the congregation. The purpose of these rituals is to diffuse the power of the Holy Ghost, previously concentrated in the speaker, among all who are present at worship. Prior to sharing his power with other members, the speaker is said to be in a most dangerous and supercharged state. If the speaker's power were not shared, it would destroy him.

In rituals of sharing and touching, the speaker steps down from the altar carrying a flower vase filled with water. He approaches a member of the church, placing his hands on one side of the vase while the member places two hands on the other side of the vase. The vase is moved up and down and from side to side several times (I was told emphatically that this is not the sign of the cross). This procedure is repeated with every member of the congregation.[7]

It is believed that the longer it takes to diffuse one's power, the greater one's spiritual claims. High-ranking members and those who aspire to higher ranks often must perform the ritual two or three times with each member of the congregation before they feel that the Holy Spirit has dissipated entirely.

After the paramount leader offers his final interpretation, there is a brief period of religious frenzy consisting of glossolalia, "shouting," and bell ringing. This final period of intensification may last from ten to fifteen minutes before the paramount leader calls for benediction. Benediction marks a period of contemplation and is followed by announcements from the floor concerning upcoming baptisms, mourning ceremonies, and joint worship services with other churches. A period of silence is observed both before and after announcements. No one is permitted to speak until all congregants are outside the church building. Placement of announcement at this juncture of worship is of consequence since many announcements are controversial and such placement allows no forum for debate.

Flexibility of worship permits leaders to make additions to the basic service. Embellishments may include sacrifice of a chicken, exorcism, ritual meals, Islamic or Hindu healing rites, confession, or private consultations with the pastor. For the most part, embellishments occur either before or after regular service, and under no circumstances are embellishments allowed to change the basic order of ceremonies. If, for example, a leader feels that he must perform animal sacrifice, this is done after the close of the regular church service. Members leave the church building, wait ten minutes or more, and then begin preparations for sacrifice, which is always held outside the church—usually in another community. To be most effective, sacrifice should be performed on another day of the week. Some Baptists who sponsor Shango rituals perform "African" drumming both before and after service, but never during the actual service itself. In this way, leaders are able to separate rituals borrowed from other traditions. Such embellishments are considered very important because they serve to differentiate one church from another and, more important, are believed to be a means of attracting new members.

Baptism and Mourning Rites

In the eyes of most Baptists, two rituals distinguish them from all other religious bodies: baptism and mourning rites. In regard to these rituals, few embellishments are permitted. Baptism and mourning ceremonies observed in 1976, 1978, and 1982 have much in common with earlier descriptions of these ceremonies provided by Herskovits and Herskovits, and Simpson. This illustrates how conservative Baptists are in the observance of these rites; Henney reported in 1974 on the Baptists of St. Vincent, and the Herskovitses' data are over forty years old.

All candidates are expected to receive religious instruction of varying intensity prior to baptism. Instruction may last from several hours to several months, although one week is considered the normal period of preparation. Teachings consist of Bible readings, prayer, and a type of divination known as "proving." In "proving," candidates are asked to close their eyes, open the Bible, and pick a random verse. Verses thus chosen are said to reveal a candidate's readiness for baptism. In addition, these verses serve as a basis for later instruction.

Church leaders claim to "scrutinize" candidates for baptism rigorously. Ideally, a leader should not perform baptism rites without a teacher's approval; however, in practice teachers are seldom able to deny anyone participation in the rites. Churches constantly seek new members and rarely turn anyone away.

Church elders are aware that if a candidate experiences too much resistance at one church, he or she will readily become a candidate at another. Several Curepe leaders indicated that under certain conditions they would be willing to baptize a candidate without a period of prior instruction.

Preparations for baptism are no longer as rigorous as the preparations described by Herskovits and Herskovits in 1947. At the time of the Herskovitses' research, leaders and teachers imposed restrictions on personal behavior prior to the rite, including demands for sexual abstinence and fasting. This is no longer the case because candidates for mourning and baptism come from more distant villages, and these restrictions are often difficult to enforce due to increased geographical mobility. However, geographical mobility does not provide a complete explanation for this change. Restrictions have also become much more lax in St. Vincent, where many Baptists continue to attend services in their own communities.

After completion of initial instruction, a candidate is presented to the paramount leader for baptism. Usually a date is chosen when there are other candidates for the rite. This saves the leader considerable time and expense, and is also thought to make the rite more enjoyable for the candidate.

Most often, rites of baptism begin on a Saturday evening and continue until Sunday morning. In recent years, some leaders have offered shorter ceremonies at other times. Shorter ceremonies contain all the elements of the longer ceremonies, but less time is devoted to each of the various segments. Although shorter ceremonies have been criticized in some quarters (and privately by some leaders who themselves perform the shorter ceremonies), so-called quickie baptisms are rapidly growing in popularity. One reason may be that they cost less than the traditional rite. Another reason given is that shorter ceremonies are allegedly more "healthy" for older leaders, who must supervise the rite. I suspect that there is a third reason, namely, shorter ceremonies serve to differentiate further Spiritual Baptist ceremonies from the longer Shango ceremonies. Whatever the reason, by 1982 most Curepe baptisms were of the quickie variety.

A significant aspect of the above change is that services no longer run all night. In 1982 I observed two baptisms, one of which began at 11 A.M. and was completed at 5:30 P.M.; the other began at 1:30 P.M. and was completed at 7:30 P.M. The second baptism actually was a much shorter service than the first because the time span included two hours of travel to and from Maracas Bay for rites of immersion. In the first case, travel was unnecessary because there is a river about two hundred yards from the church building (see Photograph 5).

In the first segment of the baptism ritual, candidates are given white robes and "bands" to wrap around their heads, covering both their eyes and ears. In some churches, candidates are expected to bring their own bands, while at other churches, leaders and mothers wash used bands and provide them to candidates for a fee.

The candidate, unable to see, is led to the sanctuary and placed on the Mercy Seat, a front bench signed with mystical writings and symbols. Lighted candles, symbolizing the Holy Ghost, are placed in the candidate's hands. Candidates are expected to hold these burning candles for several hours, and it is believed that as long as the Holy Ghost is with them they will not be burned by the hot wax. In the early part of the ritual, church leaders attempt to make the Holy Ghost manifest in the candidate by utilizing techniques of "adoption" as well as by singing, hand clapping, and prayer.

Those researchers who have interpreted baptism and mourning ceremonies solely in terms of sensory deprivation have greatly underestimated the degree of physical contact between candidates and members of the congregation.[8] For much of the rite, candidates receive a barrage of stimuli. Bands may interfere with one's sight, but not with one's senses of smell, touch, taste, or hearing. In services I observed, there seemed to be little monotony for candidates. They performed a variety of activities including singing, marching, standing, sitting, sleeping, eating, and drinking.

Between six o'clock in the evening, when the candidate is placed on the Mercy Seat, and dawn, when actual rites of baptism usually take place, members of the congregation offer "words of consolation" to the candidate. Most congregants take this opportunity to tell candidates about their own baptisms. Members present are also allowed to take candidates for walks, get them drinks, or take them to the church latrine. Many church members go home for the night at eleven, and in some churches candidates are allowed to sleep (either in the mourning chamber or on church pews) from midnight to five o'clock in the morning.

Candidates are awakened at 5:00 A.M. and begin preparations for baptisms. They are removed from the church and taken to a body of "moving" water, usually a river, where rites of immersion occur. In many churches baptism takes place at dawn. Candidates who have been baptized previously in another denomination are separated from those candidates who have never been baptized. The former individuals are "re-washed" (sprinkled with water), while the latter individuals are completely immersed in the water three times: once "in the name of God the Father," once "in the name of God the Son," and once "in the name of God the Holy Ghost."[9] The initial dunking is considered the most efficacious. In many respects, immersion rites parallel baptisms among the London Baptists and other standard Baptist denominations.

After immersion, candidates remove their bands and their wet clothing. They are provided with dry robes and return to the church to be anointed with oil and to receive further instruction. Following hymns, exhortations, glossolalia, and prayer, the baptism service comes to a close. Three regular baptisms observed lasted fourteen, sixteen, and fourteen hours, respectively.

Elements from baptism rites also play a very large part in the mourning ceremony.[10] A major difference is one of duration. While candidates for baptism may wear their bands for as long as sixteen hours, mourners wear their bands for up to three weeks. Candidates for the mourning ceremony are scrutinized less carefully than are candidates for baptism. It is assumed that all mourners have been baptized previously, but no attempts are made to verify this.

While Baptists can be cynical about many of their rituals, most Baptists take mourning rites very seriously. They approach mourning with some ambivalence. On the one hand, it is the most sacred of all church rites; on the other hand, it is believed to be potentially dangerous. If one does not take his or her mourning vows seriously, he or she may become insane or, as the Baptists say, "travel in the wrong direction." Usually if a mourner travels in the wrong direction, his or her leader is blamed. Sometimes, however, the leader is able to shift blame to the mourner, an attendant, or some other church member.

Fewer church members attend an entire mourning ceremony than are present for the entire baptism rite. Still, mourners are never left alone, and there is a great deal of sensory stimulation for participants. In some churches, observance of mourning rites is very lax. After public aspects of the ceremony have been completed, Baptist leaders sometimes allow mourners to take off their bands and to smoke, talk, and laugh with friends. Formalities are difficult to maintain because mourners and their supervisors are usually close friends outside the mourning chamber.

The purpose of the mourning ceremony is to induce visions or dreams that are believed to reveal one's "true" rank within the faith. Baptists recognize twenty-two specialized ranks, and each rank is associated with specific duties:

Provers interpret spiritual writing. They test the powers of pointers and teachers and may be called upon to test the sincerity of candidates for baptism.

Preachers are authorities in the interpretation of scripture. They are called upon whenever conflicts arise over the interpretation of a particular passage. They also may give words of consolation and admonition at baptism and mourning ceremonies.

Shepherds care for children. They remove disruptive youngsters from the place of worship and may suggest a particular child as a candidate for baptism.

Captains care for the church building. They are responsible for all maintenance and suggest possible church improvements. They delegate many of their duties to other church members. A major responsibility is making certain services begin and end on time.

Pointers help direct mourning rites. They aid mourners in obtaining good visions, and are said to direct a mourner's dreams by prayers to God the Holy Ghost.

Bell Ringers drive out evil spirits in the vicinity of the church building by clanging bells and strewing perfumed water. They perform these acts both before and after ceremonies.

Water Carriers lead candidates for baptism to a moving body of water, where immersion takes place. They may also, at the discretion of church leaders, strew perfumed water during worship services, especially if a member is believed to be possessed by a Shango deity.

Postmen carry messages to distant leaders. They may be asked to arrange pilgrimages. During worship, they sometimes aid in the interpretation of glossolalia and the reading of tracts.

Healers perform various healing rituals and pray for the well-being of all church members. Their focus is on prevention. If a member of the congregation becomes ill, it is often assumed that the healer has neglected his or her duties.

Divers keep members from straying from the church. If a soul is lost the diver must try to recover it. Their major responsibility is to visit former members of the church and to try to win them back.

Watchmen help church visitors find a seat and make them feel comfortable. Watchmen are given responsibility for recruitment and are always on the lookout for new members.

Surveyors test the water prior to baptism. They ascertain that the water is "clean" (free of orisha) and at times may be asked to recommend suitable baptism sites.

Nurses tend candidates in the mourning room. They are under direct supervision of Spiritual mothers, and watch candidates in six- or eight-hour shifts. Nurses prepare whatever food is served in the mourning room and guide the mourner to the latrine.

Teachers recommend candidates for baptism. They provide instruction to candidates, often selecting children for baptism. Theoretically, candidates for baptism may not be accepted into the faith without a teacher's approval.

Leaders direct services of mourning and baptism. They are the final authority in the interpretation of tracts and provide words of consolation during the ceremony.

Mothers direct physical aspects of the mourning ceremony. They set the date, make certain nurses will be available to supervise the rite, buy necessary provisions, collect money from the candidate, and redistribute this among their helpers.

Sisters are the lowest-ranking female members of the faith. They are expected to obey commands from superiors, labor for the good of the church, buy pilgrimage tickets and contribute to church assessments, and attend worship regularly.

Brothers are the lowest-ranking male members of the faith. They, too, are expected to obey commands, attend worship, and give generously of their time and resources.

Warriors, Commanders, Inspectors, and *Judges* are the highest-ranking church members. They settle disputes among other high-ranking church members, oversee mission programs, and serve as a court of appeal on matters of church policy. A limited number of persons attain these ranks. No one from the Curepe community occupied the rank of judge or inspector in 1978.

Some ranks within the church are considered to be at the same level. Mourners complain that what appears to be a great deal of advancement within a church is actually horizontal rather than vertical mobility (see Table 2). Horizontal mobility is most prevalent in large and well-established churches, while vertical mobility is much more rapid in newer churches. In both older and newer churches, other factors that come into play in determining advancement include the number of leadership positions vacant, age structure of the congregation, and the perceived loyalty of the mourner.

I contend that previous researchers have overstated the connection between visions obtained in the mourning ceremony and church rank. Baptists note that there is no one-to-one correspondence between visions and ranks, that advancement is never based on visions per se but on visions as they are interpreted by church leaders. Two mourners may claim identical visions yet earn very different ranks, as happened three times during my fieldwork. In fact, leaders emphasize that experienced mourners frequently obtain identical visions. Ward and Beaubrun state: "More experienced mourners who have come to build on previous experiences tend to have qualitatively different hallucinations. For example, these pilgrims are more likely to see themselves among a flock of sheep, gathering fish in a large net or walking up the road to the celestial city—a set of pseudoperceptions which obviously reflect greater symbolic significance."[11] Ward and Beaubrun's observation was noted much more succinctly by one informant who flatly stated: "Experienced mourners lie."

Table 2
HIERARCHY OF MERIT, MT. TABOR SPIRITUAL BAPTIST CHURCH

Level	Rank
10	Judge
9	Inspector
8	Commander
7	Warrior
6	Teacher-Pointer
5	Captain-Prover-Diver
4	Mother-Leader-Prover
3	Surveyor-Shepherd-Postman-Watchman-Nurse-Preacher
2	Water Fetcher-Carrier
1	Sister-Brother

It is true not only that mourners may falsify their visions but that leaders themselves play a part in this fabrication. At the conclusion of each day, church leaders meet with each mourner to discuss visions and dreams received over the past twenty-four hours.[12] Mourners are instructed to "discard" some dreams, while they are told to "save" other dreams "in their hearts." The latter dreams are often written down so they can be recited during public worship the following Sunday.

When a mourner speaks publicly about his or her visions, the public statements do not represent exactly their visionary experiences but are edited and condensed versions of what transpired in the mourning chamber. It is claimed that public statements account for only about 5 or 10 percent of what happens "on the ground." The remainder of one's visions are to be forgotten or saved for oneself.

Public statements by mourners, also known as "tracts," are carefully rehearsed with church elders prior to presentation. Common themes emerge in the construction of final public statements.[13] In the following examples note the stress on generosity, foreign places, and the sudden appearance of familiar figures from the local congregation.

I am walking by a stream. I am thirsty, but do not have a cup. A man . . . a Chinese . . . offers me a cup. I take the cup. I dip into the water and take a drink, but I still am thirsty. He tells me to keep the cup, but I give it back to him saying others may come after me who will have need of it. Father, Son, and Holy Ghost. . . . I go travelling in Africa. . . . A child comes to me with a sore foot. I put a bandage on the child's foot. The mother comes. . . . she scolds me for bandaging the child. She says I am wasting time. I am travelling in China. . . . I come to a giant tree, there is a man in the tree. It is Brother Bertie. Brother Bertie gives me a silver chalice. . . . Father, Son and Holy Ghost. . . . Amen.

I am in Africa. . . . along the road comes a strange man who knows me. I am frightened because I do not know him. He questions me askin' me why I am travellin'. I say that I is seekin' wisdom, truth and knowledge. He says I is a liar and must repent and be a seeker of justice. I tell him no. An animal appears, a leopard, the man runs away. Father, Son and Holy Ghost. . . . I come to a river and trees. Flowers are along the side of the river. The river is deep and I am falling into it. I can't stop myself from falling. Mother R. appears and she pulls me up. I feel safe and am glad to see her. Father, Son and Holy Ghost. . . . I am in Africa again. . . . it is dark and someone hands me a lighted candle. . . . I take it but give it back saying that someone else may come along who needs it more than I. I hear drums and bells and follow them to a clearing in the forest. Father, Son and Holy Ghost. . . . Amen.

I am in China. I am floating in a river. My boat is sinkin'. Leader R. tells me to come to shore. There is a crowd of people—strangers—they ask me why I am on the river. I say I am a seeker. Father, Son and Holy Ghost. . . . I am fishing but the fish will not come to my net. I try another spot and my net is overflowing. My heart is filled with gladness because I see Jesus on the shore. He waves to me. Father, Son and Holy Ghost. . . . I am travellin' to Jerusalem. I see the gates of the city. They are made of gold. Outside is garbage. I must clear it. . . . I work hard. . . . it is clean. A man gives me a silver coin. I drop it on the ground. When I pick it up I am standin' amidst a flock of sheep. I am blessed. Father, Son and Holy Ghost. . . . Amen.

In the first two public statements, collected at different churches, both candidates seek to demonstrate that they are worthy of advancement. In the first case, the mourner turns down a cup, even though she is thirsty, while in the second case, the mourner turns down a lighted candle even though it is dark. This shows a willingness to put the needs of others above one's own desires—an important quality for those who would occupy leadership positions. In both of these tracts, church members make appearances offering support and advice. Some leaders say that they distrust mourners who include them in visions. It is often seen as attempted flattery. In the third tract, Jesus himself makes an appearance and waves to the mourner. This vision, if accepted by the congregation, would greatly increase the mourner's prestige in the church.

The words "Father, Son and Holy Ghost" serve to separate visions obtained on separate days of the rite. Entire days or weeks may be left out of tracts at the discretion of the mourner or church leaders. In the three tracts presented above, mourners reported on two, three, and three days, respectively, of a one-week ceremony.

Similarities of reported visions are determined on at least two levels. A leader may encourage all candidates to articulate their experiences in similar terms, or candidates may elect to mourn under a particular leader because he has a reputation for "directing" participants to experience certain visions. In one Curepe church, for example, all mourners "travel" to China, while at another church in San Juan, all mourners travel to Africa. One mourner, while recounting her visions at the San Juan church, began to speak of visions that had taken place in India. Her leader, who had a reputation for sending candidates to Africa, allowed her to speak of India for about a minute before interrupting in a booming voice, "And then you were in Africa!" The mourner promptly complied and changed the locale of her vision. At the same session, another mourner spoke of a vision that had taken place in China. She, too, was interrupted and forced to change her locale to Africa.

In some churches, candidates are told what church rank they have received in the final day of the ceremony, prior to public recitation of visions. In other churches, candidates are not told of their new ranks until after the entire ceremony, including presentation of tracts, has been completed. In one church, the paramount leader waits three full weeks after the conclusion of the rite before he announces formally a candidate's new rank.

Each member of the congregation, including visitors, is expected to comment on every mourner's tracts. Comments are supposedly intended to illuminate the mourner's new responsibilities within the church; however, since tracts are incomplete and mourners often keep their most important visions to themselves, it is very difficult for congregants to offer illumination. Most members make vague statements to obviate the fact that they have no idea which rank the candidate has earned. Typical statements include "The mourner seems to have travelled far" or "It is gratifying when a pilgrim has seen so much."

Some portions of individual tracts are relatively unambiguous to better informed members of the congregation. In the first tract, for example, the mourner stated that she was scolded for bandaging a child. Before going into the mourning chamber, this woman occupied the rank of shepherd. One implication of her statement is that she is no longer to be a "tender of children" because her spiritual powers are far greater. In her former rank, she was "wastin' time."

The second candidate had been accused of mourning for selfish reasons. She was involved in a legal dispute, and some church members believed that she went to mourn solely in order to win her court case.[14] In her tracts she answered her critics directly, stating that she had higher aspirations, namely, seeking after "wisdom, truth and knowledge."

In addition to its association with church rank, the mourning ceremony is also considered a way of combating orisha and bad luck. Misfortune and illness are often interpreted as calls to mourn. It is widely believed that the rite has curative powers and that if one enters the mourning ceremony sick, he or she will emerge from the ceremony in a healthy state.

Baptists participate in mourning rites frequently. Loyal church members are expected to mourn at least once every three years. Mourning ceremonies may be initiated at the request of the candidate or by church leaders. While many members volunteer for the rite, many other members wait for leaders to approach them and request their participation. When a leader approaches a member, this almost insures the member's advancement within the faith. Self-selection, on the other hand, is always riskier, since leaders do not have as strong an obligation to promote candidates they do not select.

Healing Rites

Members of the faith consider healing rites separate from all other religious activities. These rites occur either before or after regular service or, more frequently, at private ceremonies held on other days of the week. Usually only close friends and relatives attend. Not all Baptist leaders perform healing rites, and those who do emphasize that their healing skills are not dependent on their participation in Baptist ceremonies. It is recognized, however, that a practitioner's healing powers may be enhanced by participation in Baptist rituals.

Healers are not accorded high status within the faith. Three reasons are given to account for this: (1) that healing is women's work, (2) that healing is a "test" of God's power, and (3) that healing is primarily the work of the two lower-ranking members of the Trinity—God the Son and God the Holy Ghost. The first explanation, that it is women's work, is not consistent with observed behavior, since many male leaders do perform healing rites. Also, it is noted that women are given responsible positions in Baptist services—for example, they supervise mourners and may scrutinize candidates for baptism. The second explanation, derived from the Biblical injunction "Thou shouldst not test the Lord thy God," is also inconsistent with observed behavior. Church leaders test the Lord almost daily in their economic decisions. The third explanation, that healing is primarily the work of God the Son and God the Holy Ghost, is somewhat more satisfactory. In the eyes of many Baptists, healing may be unimportant because it deals with the body and the spirit instead of the mind. No wisdom is conferred by healing rites.

While many Baptist leaders refuse to perform rites of healing, most will perform rites for close friends or to win new converts to their churches. It is common for a leader to train his wife in healing techniques, thereby enabling him to participate in healing without diminishing his status.

According to Baptist etiology, illness is caused by an imbalance of fluids within the body brought on by spirit intrusion. Two major healing techniques are utilized in dealing with spirit intrusion: "adoption" and anointment. Of these two techniques, adoption is considered the most effective cure for use on nonbelievers, while anointment is considered the most effective treatment for use on fellow Baptists. Touching plays a part in both techniques. In adoption healers rub the afflicted's chest and abdominal region, and in anointment healers rub the victim's head and limbs.

These techniques differ from the techniques of other native healers. Healers in the Rada cult, for example, enter into a trance state before they are able to diagnose a client's problem.[15] Baptists insist, to the contrary, that it is unnecessary for healers to enter a trance to diagnose illness. Some Baptists contend that it is not necessary for a healer to know the cause of an illness in order to cure it. Adoption and anointment are thought to be sufficient cures for all afflictions.

In extremely difficult cases, Baptist healers may prescribe herbal medicines, a practice also common to other groups within the culture. Herbal medicines merely supplement the healing techniques described above. Clients never go directly to Baptist healers for herbal medicines since most Trinidadians have a good knowledge of herbs and do not seek outside help until home remedies and patent medicines have failed them.

Some Spiritual Baptist women who make their living raising and selling herbal medicines are known as "bush ladies." Baptists emphasize that this is their profession only and has little bearing on their life in the faith. Being a bush lady is considered very much the same as working in a drug store, and many bush ladies contend that herbal remedies and patent medicines are identical. The major differences between bush and patent medicines, according to one informant, is that patent medicines cost more. Murine, a patent medicine to clear the eyes, is said to contain the same ingredients as English plantain, a common herbal remedy. Bush ladies frequently complain that "drug companies in the United States steals our medicine and gets rich."

Differentiation between bush ladies and healers among the Spiritual Baptists of Trinidad is very similar to the distinction made in Haiti between *traitment* and *wangu*. Herskovits noted the same pattern in West Africa: "In West Africa, those who deal in herbs, roots and other curatives are invariably differentiated from those whose cures from illness and other less mundane evils come from supernatural powers."[16] Among the

Baptists, as in Africa, those who deal in herbs are not believed to cure on the basis of supernatural powers.

Since herbal remedies are neither unique to the Baptist faith nor a focus of Baptist healing rites, it is ironic that most existing data on herbal medicines in the Caribbean are taken from Baptist informants. Both Simpson and Wong relied on the assistance of Baptist bush ladies in compiling their native pharmacopoeias.[17] What data I have gathered on herbal medicine are also taken from a Baptist informant, Mother R.

Mother R. learned her trade from an East Indian neighbor long before she began attending Baptist rites. Knowledge of herbs is usually passed from mother to daughter, but in this case the bush lady had no children or close relatives willing to learn, so she offered her knowledge to Mother R. for $25TT. According to several informants, it was comparatively easy to buy medical knowledge during the 1930s, providing that one had money in the middle of the Great Depression, and it did not make any difference how such knowledge was obtained. Since Trinidadians do not differentiate among bush ladies, all are considered to be equally adept at teaching their trade.

Whereas all "bush" is considered equal, healing in Trinidad is much more complex, and opinions vary as to the efficacy of various healers. Patent medicines and herbal medicines are usually the remedy of first choice. When these medicines fail, other alternatives are explored, including Rada healers, Protestant ministers, and Catholic priests. Medical doctors and obeahmen, because they are the most expensive alternative, are frequently the healers of last resort. A local doctor told me that he rarely sees Spiritual Baptist patients until after it is too late to begin effective treatment. Although Trinidad has a system of socialized medicine, individuals must enter the hospital in Port of Spain to receive free medical attention. Most Curepe residents are reluctant to do this and would prefer to pay a private practitioner within their own community rather than make the journey to Port of Spain.

In the course of my research, I was very surprised by the large number of Spiritual Baptists who consult with Protestant ministers—Presbyterian, Methodist, or Adventist—and Catholic priests before seeking help from their own pastor. In time I learned that according to Baptist belief illness is a result of not living up to one's obligations to the church and is interpreted as a sign of God's disfavor. A Baptist cannot seek help from his or her pastor without demonstrating a lack of spiritual worth. To avoid this, many Baptists seek help at other churches where they are able to preserve a degree of anonymity.

Illness, as mentioned earlier, is believed to be caused by an imbalance of fluids within the body brought on by spirit intrusion. The focus of Baptist healing, therefore, is to restore balance. This concern has much in common with what anthropologists working in other parts of the world, particularly Central America, have labeled the "hot and cold theory of disease."[18] A major difference is that Trinidadians do not refer directly to the four body fluids of humoral medicine (blood, phlegm, yellow bile, and black bile), nor do they associate hot medicines with dryness and cold medicines with wetness, as is common elsewhere. Baptist concerns with balance may, in the opinion of one researcher, be closer to homeopathic medicine than the Greek humoral theory of Hippocrates, which has greatly influenced medical practice in the Spanish New World.[19] While Trinidad was a Spanish colony for nearly three hundred years, settlements were small, and Spanish influence does not seem to have been pronounced.[20]

On the whole, Baptist healers are supremely confident in their abilities but recognize that the results of treatment are always uncertain. Many factors affecting successful treatment are beyond human control. In this, healing practices have much in common with Baptist rites of purification. Baptist attitudes toward healing and purification are very similar. Sometimes, it is noted, healing and purification rites are successful; other times, these rites are not successful and must be repeated.

All Baptist rites decribed in this chapter are characterized by indeterminancy. Baptists believe that man's dominion over the spirit world is severely limited, and relations with the spirit world are poorly defined; for example, anointment oil, as an extension of God the Son should have dominion over orisha— but this is not always the case. Powers of God the Son may be counteracted by powers of God the Father, who does not always favor man in his battles with the spirit world. At other times, however, God the Son will prevail. There is no way of knowing beforehand, according to my informants, what the outcome of healing rites—or any other rituals—will be.

Leadership Decisions and Ritual Change

While mourning, baptism, and healing rites have remained very much as they were described by earlier researchers, there have been a number of changes in the major public ceremony, as was indicated earlier. The greatest number of changes in the faith have taken place within the context of regular worship. Americanist scholars, most notably Roger Bastide, recently have become very much concerned with ritual change. The most common interpretation, either expressed or implied in the writings of Bastide and his followers, is that many religious traditions (formerly separate) are blending in the New World and that each distinctive tradition, whether from Europe, Africa, or Asia, is undergoing a transformation that will result in a new religious synthesis or coagulation.[21] In recent years, this process has been documented for Catholicism and vodun in Haiti,[22] and for Hinduism and Christianity in Martinique.[23]

Trinidad's Spiritual Baptists, however, appear to be somewhat of an exception to this process. Although Baptists do adopt elements from other religious traditions (Shango, Hinduism, and Islam), they also attempt to provide each borrowed element with its own spatial and temporal context in order to avoid the confusion or blending of religious traditions. Each religious practice is said to have its greatest efficacy within its own context; for example, Hindu elements are segregated from African elements, and both Hindu and African elements are separated from Baptist (Christian) elements. Since each element is believed to be most powerful in its context of origin, any other context is believed to result in a lessening of power.

Ritual change among the Baptists must be understood as a conscious process. It is a product of rational decision making on the part of an individual church leader.[24] A leader decides, often for pragmatic reasons, to make specific changes in the order of worship, to add embellishments, or to borrow from other religious traditions. While broader processes of syncretism and interpenetration may occur, individually planned ritual change has by far the greatest impact on the faith.

Rituals are added frequently, and processes of accretion appear to follow closely what Bastide has termed the "principle of juxtaposition." In juxtaposition, rituals from diverse traditions may be performed within the same religious service, but these rituals must be separated spatially and or temporally from one another. The purpose of juxtaposition is to add rituals in their purest possible form, and the results in Baptist worship are a virtual mosaic of African, Hindu, Islamic, Protestant, Catholic, and Pentecostal rites within a single service.

Bastide claims that juxtaposition is a comparatively rare form of ritual change, since most religions accumulate rites in order to fortify and enrich themselves. In most religions, he contends, rites from various traditions are mixed and or coagulated to "make each rite more efficacious."[25] This is not the case in Baptist worship. Baptists do not believe that an accumulated rite is as strong in the Baptist context as it was in its original context. Leaders are very conscientious in their borrowing so as to maintain rituals as they are believed to have been before being adopted into Baptist worship. In their performance of rites, Baptist leaders, in the words of Leader D., attempt to be "more Hindu than them Indians, more African than them Africans, and more Pentecostal than them Pentecostals." In fact, Baptist leaders are so conservative in this respect that they often maintain selected rites long after the model religious groups have abandoned them.

Juxtaposition influences greatly the structure and duration of Baptist rituals. Because more items are added than are dropped from ceremonies, services tend to be lengthened to accommodate ritual change. Also, because an independent context must be established for each added ritual, Baptist worship services may sometimes appear segmented and or compartmentalized.

Evidence for juxtaposition may be noted in the physical layouts of church compounds. Most churches consist of at least three separate ritual areas, and some Curepe churches have as many as six separate structures on their property, including shrines. For those Baptists who are involved also in Shango, additional buildings are necessary because Shango is never held on the grounds of a Baptist church, and most Curepe churches maintain separate Shango "palais" (ceremonial centers) in neighboring San Juan or Tunapuna. San Juan and Tunapuna churches, in turn, often maintain their Shango palais in Curepe (see Appendix).

The main buildings of churches believed to be prosperous are often no larger than those of poorer churches, but prosperous churches have more outbuildings. The wealthiest church in Curepe maintains a separate mourning chamber (about one hundred feet from the main building), a latrine, a small guesthouse for overnight visitors, four shrines (one large enough to accommodate twenty people), and an office for the paramount leader. Poorer Curepe churches, unable to afford a separate chamber for mourning or separate shrines, erect partitions so as to separate various ritual functions within the main building. All churches have separate offices for their leaders and separate latrines. When a church is unable to provide its leader with an office on church grounds, the leader is expected to conduct church business from his home. Under no conditions are business and worship supposed to mix.

One church, lacking money for a separate mourning chamber and separate shrines, constructed its mourning room behind the altar and placed shrines in small cubicles in the back of the church. Another church built a large lean-to structure to accommodate mourners and maintains three open-air shrines. Leaders of both these churches plan to construct additional outbuildings.

Shrines, whether or not enclosed, may be dedicated to any deity. Even those churches opposed to Shango will permit some African shrines as long as these are outside the main building.

Catholic saints, as mentioned previously, are accorded similar status to African gods. Saints' shrines often take the form of brightly colored statuettes that are never allowed in the main church building. Curepe Baptists do not appear to favor any particular saint. In 1977, Saint Francis, Saint Barbara, and Saint Jude were represented in the community. There were also two shrines to the Virgin Mary.

Shrines to saints and Shango deities are constructed and maintained, for the most part, by individuals. Many Baptists keep shrines in their homes and also construct a shrine at the church to share whatever benefits they feel they have received from the saints with other members of the congregation.

The most recent outbuilding to appear as part of the church complex is a separate building for Pentecostal-type exorcism. These buildings, usually opposite the mourning chamber, replicate in miniature the Pentecostal church in Curepe, complete with sound system, vestments, and so forth. Although the building for exorcism is used only once or twice a month, Baptists do not transfer ritual paraphernalia from one ritual setting to another. Churches, in this case, maintain two sound systems and two altars. In the eyes of Baptist leaders, maintenance of juxtaposition takes precedence over the expense of duplication.

There is considerable spatial separation within the Baptist sanctuary itself. Christian ritual paraphernalia including crosses, chromolithographs of Jesus, the chariot wheel, and vestments are on a raised platform in the front of the church, while Hindu and Islamic paraphernalia are relegated to the back of the church. Where leaders have incorporated both Hindu and Catholic rituals, saints' shrines may be placed at the rear of the church, and chromolithographs of the Hindu deities are confined to the left wall.

Some Baptists spatially separate African deities, Catholic saints, and the Bible in their own homes by dedicating a separate room to each. Because of the cramped quarters of many Baptist dwellings, a full room devoted to each religious tradition is sometimes out of the question, and some members place room dividers between various household shrines.

While spatial juxtaposition appears to be the preferred mode of ritual separation, Baptists attempt to separate ritual elements temporally as well. In some churches drumming, which is usually associated with African (Shango) rites, may be performed before rites of purification have begun. At this time, it is also permissible, but not desirable, for individuals to become possessed by Shango deities. In the context of regular Baptist worship, however, such behavior is deemed to be a serious breach of etiquette.

Some Baptists, especially those with Shango involvement, practice animal sacrifice. These rites are never performed on church grounds, and to be most effective should not be performed on the same day as Baptist ceremonies. Sacrificial rites, utilizing chickens or goats, tend to occur in remote areas like the waterfall at Maracas, Maracas Bay, Manzanilla, or the National Forest.[26] Participants are sworn to secrecy, and some Baptists suggest that sacrifice may be illegal, although there are no records of any leader's having been arrested on that charge.

In some church-sponsored journeys, members carried live chickens with them on the bus. Those who carried chickens were left off at Manzanilla or Maracas, while other church members continued to another destination. I believe that those who left the bus performed rites of animal sacrifice. While I have never personally attended an animal sacrifice, I have noted that the aforementioned chickens were not present on the return journey. Baptist leaders were unwilling to confirm my suspicion that a sacrifice had taken place; however, several leaders did remark that if one participates in animal sacrifice, he or she should not participate in Baptist worship on the same day.

Two or three times a year some Baptist leaders sponsor communal meals. These meals are considered to be a part of the Protestant tradition—borrowed, I am told, from Methodist and Presbyterian church suppers—and not in any way related to the Catholic mass. Meals generally follow the regular service, although at times they may be held independently of service and on other days of the week. Nearly everyone who attends Baptist worship is invited to the communal meal afterward; in addition, some individuals are invited who do not participate in worship on a regular basis. Landlords and politicians are frequent guests.

The menu usually consists of *roti* (an Indian pancake stuffed with curried meat and potato), *peleau* (a rice and meat casserole cooked over a charcoal fire), and yams, eddo, breadfruit, cassava bread, and figs. These are standard Trinidadian party foods, easy to prepare and relatively inexpensive. Each participant in the feast is expected to bring something, and most participants bring much more food than they personally are able to consume.

Food is never served immediately following a service. There is sometimes a break of an hour and a half between the close of a service and the beginning of the meal. Members who live close to the church go home, change their clothes, and return later for the feast. Those living some distance away visit area snack bars for a quick snack.

While there are some religious overtones to communal meals, the meals are understood to be primarily secular and/or social occasions. Devout Baptists pray before eating, but other forms of religious expression are not encouraged. Communal meals are often considered an appropriate context for the discussion of church business.

Two other types of communal meals are sponsored in some Baptist circles. Baptists involved in Shango sponsor feasts known as "feeding the children" in honor of African deities,[27] while Baptists who maintain saints' shrines sponsor feasts known as "Thanksgivings." Both types of feasts are usually held in the sponsor's home. A table is covered with a white cloth and various objects are placed on the table, including a vase of flowers, a glass of water, a bottle of milk, a bottle of rum, a bottle of olive oil, a jar of honey, candles, bread, cookies, roasted corn, oranges, plums, bananas, figs, candy, and soda. After prayer, Bible readings, and hymns, food is distributed to all worshippers, with special attention to children, who consume most of the cookies, candy, fruit, corn, and soda. As each child leaves, he or she is given a small sack of food to take home.

"Feeding of the children" is followed by a communal meal in which more expensive—"exotic"—foods are served to the adults present. One such meal included canned tuna fish, Kellogg's corn flakes, and imported Danish cheeses. In addition, each participant was given a piece of goat meat, an apple, and rice.

Relations with the gods in these contexts are much more manipulative than is generally common in Baptist rituals. Shango members say that they make '*susu* with African gods, while in "Thanksgivings" members make bargains, known as *promesas*, with the saints. African deities and Catholic saints are expected to honor their contracts with devotees. If gods do not honor requests, they will not receive a feast the following year.

Within the Baptist service itself, temporal separation is very prevalent. Breaks in the service, some lasting for as long as fifteen minutes, serve to separate various ritual traditions and, it is believed, to preserve borrowed ritual forms intact. The longest breaks often separate traditions that Baptists feel are close enough to one another to be confused; for example, Protestant and Catholic versions of the Lord's Prayer are separated by a two- or three-minute break during which some Baptists actually leave the church building.

In analyzing tapes of Baptist rites, it is possible to detect considerable temporal separation. Many breaks appear as lulls in the tape between various worship segments. In approximately forty hours of tapes, I have identified over four hundred separate breaks. Some breaks occur in rapid succession; for example, in one church after a seven-minute break between a New Testament reading and an Old Testament reading, someone recited several passages from the Koran, thereby necessitating another four-minute break. Most leaders try to space breaks evenly throughout the three-to-six hour service.

Rituals at the center pole—associated in some churches with African tribal religion—are always followed by a break before worship may continue at the altar—associated with Christian worship. There are, as mentioned previously, rites of touching at the conclusion of illumination and prayer, and whenever worship is transferred from the center pole to the altar, these rites are extended.

The longest break, fifteen minutes, occurs when a member is seized by an African spirit in the midst of a Baptist ceremony. If this occurs within a "hot" portion of the service, service is brought to a complete stop. Glossolalia and possession by African gods are not supposed to mix, and confusion is thought to be dangerous, polluting, and "an abomination to the Lord." One Curepe leader attempted to cope with this situation by sending everyone away, repeating intensive rites of purification, and beginning service again two hours later. Many members felt that this was an extreme measure, and that he should have sent only the possessed away, performed rites of purification, and resumed service within the hour.

Prayers to God the Son, God the Father, and God the Holy Ghost are temporally separated from one another during ceremonies. In some churches individuals pray to the three members of the Trinity from different locations behind the altar. This is not followed rigidly in all congregations and, even where it is practiced, is not practiced consistently. Gaps between prayers to members of the Trinity are short (less than a minute) and are followed by recitation of the Twenty-Third Psalm ("The Lord is my Shepherd") for God the Father, a recitation of the Lord's Prayer for God the Son, or a recitation of Matthew 18, the feast of the Pentecost, for God the Holy Ghost. Recitations serve to "prepare the way for worship."

Baptists also separate God the Father, God the Son, and God the Holy Ghost in rites of purification. The three members of the Trinity are signified by the ringing of bells ("the voice of God the Father"), strewing of flowers ("God the Son"), and incense ("God the Holy Ghost"). Each ritual is followed by a short break of two or three minutes while preparations are made for the next phase of purification. When enough qualified leaders can be found, these three rites are sometimes performed by three individuals.

After each rite has been completed, paraphernalia associated with that rite are placed in different sections of the church. Bells are kept by the altar or at the center pole for the duration of worship, flowers are placed at the rear of the sanctuary, and incense is removed from the church building. Reasons for the latter placement may have a practical rather than a theological rationale. Most churches use a pungent balsam incense believed to be noxious to orisha and, not incidentally, also noxious to humans. Members present for fumigation bow their heads toward the ground in an attempt to escape the effects of the smoke. Once leaders are satisfied that the church has been sufficiently cleansed, incense is removed and a small electric fan, where available, is used to dissipate the smoke. Most members, it should be added, prefer to enter worship after fumigation has been completed.

The order of worship varies greatly among Curepe churches. Some leaders begin rites of purification with incense, followed by strewing of perfumed water and bell ringing, while other leaders prefer to begin purification with bell ringing and progress to fumigation. Several leaders claimed that the order of ritual is not as important as the separation of rites; for example, some leaders complete all three rites and determine that another fumigation or bell ringing is necessary. Various rituals may be performed eight or nine times before a leader is satisfied.

Among many Baptist leaders, conceptions of religious ritual have much in common with Malinowski's description of Trobriand garden magic.[28] Like the Trobrianders, Baptists believe that magical efficacy and context are inextricably linked. If a mistake is made in the performance of a ritual or an insufficient context created, rites must be repeated from their beginnings.

One advantage of compartmentalization and segmentation in Baptist worship is that it lessens the amount of ritual that must be repeated if a mistake is made. Because Baptist rituals are conducted, for the most part, from memory, mistakes are made often in the recital of Biblical passages, hymns, or the Lord's Prayer. When a mistake is made, leaders may elect to repeat the entire rite, or they may let things slide. If rites are to be repeated, they must be repeated in their entirety.

Compartmentalization keeps services from becoming unwieldy and allows leaders greater discretion in performance or nonperformance of rites. It is more than a matter of convenience, however, and sometimes it reflects a leader's experience in the faith. Baptists believe that magical power rests in two quarters: (1) the magical power of ritual itself and (2) the magical power of practitioner. Experienced leaders who are in control of their churches do not need to be as careful in their performance of the rituals as do newer leaders in the faith. Inexperienced leaders perform rites exactly as they have been taught to perform them. Meticulous attention is given to every detail of worship. Experienced leaders, on the other hand, are much more relaxed in their performances. They may skip segments of worship, forget various lines of a prayer, or misquote a Biblical passage without resorting to repetition. Leader C., for example, a paramount leader of the Mt. W. church for over forty years, rarely devotes much time to rites of purification. His rites are not elaborate—in one instance, he only scattered water in all four corners of the church—but no one has been troubled by unwanted orishas in his services. On the other hand, Leader A., who assumed leadership duties in 1976, performs rituals of purification several times before the beginning of each service. Correct performance, in his case, does not seem to be enough, for many of his parishioners are still troubled by orishas during his ceremonies.

It is tempting to suggest that younger and inexperienced leaders sometimes attempt to make up, through scrupulous adherence to traditional forms, what they may lack in terms of credentials and/or legitimacy. This may offer a partial explanation for "conservatism" observed among new leaders in the faith.

Leacock and Leacock noted in their study of the Batuque cult that "all leaders do innovate to some extent, but only after they have established a reputation for knowing the traditional way of doing things."[29] The same statement could be made for Spiritual Baptist leaders. It is also noted that senior Baptist leaders adopt new ritual from other traditions more readily than do their younger counterparts, and it is the old and not the young who are most concerned with innovation. Because the locus of magical power resides both within the rite itself and with the practitioner, experienced leaders may capture the efficacy of a borrowed rite without duplicating it perfectly. This option is not available to inexperienced leaders, who must rely on efficacy inherent in the rite itself. For junior leaders the demands of ritual borrowing are extremely rigorous because their performance must reach the highest standards of perfection. Since this would involve much time and effort, the immediate advantages of ritual borrowing are less apparent to them.

Photograph 1. Greeting Ceremony, Pilgrimage at Todd's Road

Photograph 2. Leader, Mt. St. Catherine Spiritual Baptist Church, Las Lomas

74

Photograph 3. Altar, Mt. Tabor Spiritual Baptist Church

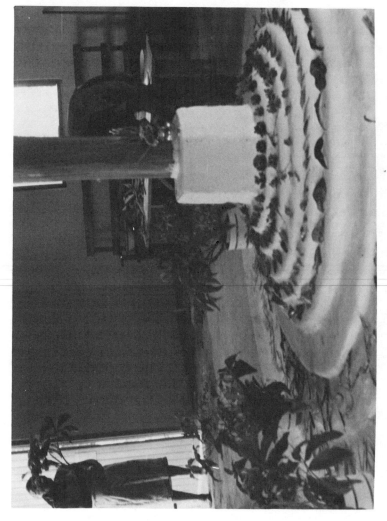

Photograph 4. Center Pole, Mt. Tabor Spiritual Baptist Church

Photograph 5. Baptism, Todd's River

4 • Leadership Roles and Church Organization

BAPTIST organization is varied and complex. No two Baptists conceive their religious organization in exactly the same way, resulting in confusion for social scientists and Baptists alike. Some analysts, notably Simpson and Henney, have confined their discussions to cult-like and sect-like aspects of the faith,[1] following distinctions made by Troeltsch and Weber.[2] Others have recognized that Baptist organization does not fit within either category and, following the precedent set by Frances Mischel in her study of Shango,[3] have labeled the Baptists a religious "group."

By far the most novel classificatory system for Caribbean religions was suggested by Hogg in his study of variants of Jamaican Revivalism.[4] He contended that there are basically two forms of religious organizations among Jamaican Revivalists: (1) monotheists, who are "sect like" in their organization, and (2) polytheists, who are "cult like" in their organization. None of the groups studied in Jamaica could qualify, according to Hogg, as churches.

A major problem with Hogg's distinction when applied to the religions of Trinidad is that most Trinidadians are polytheists. Admittedly, many of my Baptist informants profess strict monotheism but, when pressed, express fear of orisha, various African and Hindu deities, and sukoiyaas. As stated previously, Baptist notions of the Trinity are essentially polytheistic; again, when pressed, most Baptists will admit this.

Typologies developed by Troeltsch and Weber, and even those typologies developed in the Caribbean, such as Hogg's, are of limited value for understanding Baptist organization. The Baptists are far too numerous and complex to be considered a cult, are far too active politically to be considered a sect, and are far too individualistic to be considered a church in the strictest sense of the term. Troeltsch's model, developed specifically for the analysis of Christianity in Western Europe, would seem to have limited application for the study of religions outside Europe.

The basic unit of Spiritual Baptist organization is most readily identified in terms of a paramount leader, buildings, and a core of individuals who regularly participate in rituals. Baptists refer to this unit as a church; and, for want of a better term, I have adopted their usage. Churches are grouped into "denominations," but these are somewhat tenuous organizations. Each denomination has eight bishops and an archbishop, positions that are much sought after by church leaders but are not, strictly speaking, leadership positions.

The Paramount Leader

The leader of a church is called a "paramount leader." Paramount leaders are final authorities in all church affairs. Unlike members of other ranks, paramount leaders do not obtain their positions on the basis of mourning. In theory, a paramount leader may be of either sex and may have occupied any rank prior to attaining this position. In practice, however, all Curepe leaders are male, and all leaders previously occupied ranks of pointer, captain, or prover before attaining their present rank. Elsewhere on the island are a number of women who have attained, at least in theory, a rank of paramount leader. While admitting that these women wield considerable power in their respective churches, Curepe leaders claimed that they were not, truly, paramount leaders because they had little say in church "operations," could not baptize, and had to bring in an "outside" male to conduct their services.

Simpson claims that the selection of a paramount leader is "democratic,"[5] but in my experience all Baptists do not have an equal say in the selection process. All members may express their opinions, but it is the church elders, high-ranking members, who make the final decision. Whenever a vacancy occurs, many candidates are given the opportunity to compete for the position. Each candidate leads worship several times, and church members evaluate the candidate's performance and relay personal evaluations to higher-ranking members. When church elders decide that consensus has been reached, they extend an invitation to that candidate. Sometimes this process takes several years.

Baptists make a distinction between paramount leaders who are "called" to a church and paramount leaders who are "sent" to a church. If one is sent to a church, he is directed to that church on the recommendation of his bishop; whereas, if he is called to a church, he goes to that church on his own initiative. In most cases, there is no advantage in being sent by a bishop. Many churches do not recognize an individual bishop's authority, and even when a church does recognize a bishop's authority, it is not bound to accept his recommendations. In my Curepe sample, there are a large number (seven) of "called" leaders, and self-selected leaders seem to be as successful in their job searches as those leaders who are sent.

Would-be leaders prepare a list of their credentials. Such lists include previous church duties and ranks. Credentials, which resemble academic transcripts, are often professionally printed for distribution at Baptist gatherings. Another method of self-promotion is to stand up near the end of service and announce one's credentials. The most aggressive and/or ambitious would-be leaders do this even at churches not currently seeking a new paramount leader. This behavior, however, is not always regarded favorably.

Earlier studies implied that leadership roles within the faith could best be understood in terms of charismatic authority,[6] adopting Max Weber's typology in *The Sociology of Religion*. For Weber, charisma is defined as "a certain quality of an individual personality by virtue of which he is set aside from ordinary men and treated as if endowed with supernatural, superhuman, or at least exceptional powers or qualities."[7] I, too, would describe Baptist leaders as persons of exceptional ability; I did not, however, find a connection between leadership authority and manifestations of the Holy Ghost—as suggested in Herskovits and Herskovits, and Simpson. My observations suggest that there may be an inverse relationship between these two variables. Paramount leaders, for example, are never possessed by the Holy Ghost in their own churches. They are expected to remain alert and to control all aspects of worship. Their manifestations of the Holy Ghost would be interpreted by some members of their congregation as an abdication of leadership responsibilities and as a form of "self-indulgence."

Discipline and control are considered to be important qualities for leaders. Baptist leaders foster the development of "charismatic gifts" in others but are not expected to partake of these gifts themselves. A truly powerful man, according to Baptist belief, need not surrender himself to the Spirit because he is always in the Spirit; and many high-ranking members and those who aspire to high rank claim that they are able to be possessed by the Holy Ghost without ever losing control.

In matters of church authority, institutional needs often take precedence over individual qualities and experiences. In the Curepe community, I identified two distinct authority patterns, neither of which could be strictly classified as "charismatic." Two leaders had paramount authority largely because they owned their church buildings outright. Their churches were modest by Baptist standards but considerable sacrifice still had been demanded on the part of their owners. Memberships at these two churches were not large, but as one Baptist said, "They has enough to keep it goin' if nobody comes."[8] Three other Curepe leaders had authority because they had "come up through the ranks" at other churches. Although all three are men of exceptional ability, their positions are based not solely on reputation but on certificates of advancement, diplomas, and letters of recommendation from established leaders outside Curepe. They have, in effect, mourned in the best places.

Both types of leadership require years of commitment and considerable financial outlay. When a leader comes up through the ranks at an established church, he is highly regarded—especially if he has done so at an older church. As elsewhere in the world, tradition is among the strongest forms of legitimacy,[9] and Baptists rank their churches roughly according to age. Upward mobility is not easily attained in an established church because competition is fierce. At some time in their religious careers, most Baptists in Curepe have tried to obtain a high rank at an established church, usually in Port of Spain, but have failed.

On the other hand, leaders who attempt to build their own churches are accorded less prestige but exercise greater absolute authority. Leaders who hold deeds to their churches, for example, may simply ask dissident members to leave, something less easily accomplished by those who govern on the basis of "credentials." In general, there are fewer challenges to authority in these churches, and those who remain within them are, for the most part, loyal to their paramount leaders.

Long-time institutional affiliation is admired as a measure of spiritual success, and the greatest respect is accorded those who come up through the ranks in one church only. Such individuals are rare. Curepe leaders have had between five and eight institutional affiliations in the course of their careers. One informant tried to attain paramount leadership in fourteen churches before succeeding in Curepe in 1974 (he is now over seventy years old).

Leaders often overestimate the number of years they have attended their present church; for example, Leader W. claims to have come up through the ranks at Mt. Tabor Spiritual Baptist Church, which he began attending in 1946. Other members of the Mt. Tabor church point out that W. did not begin worshipping there until 1968 and that his only connection with Mt. Tabor in 1946 was that he sponsored a pilgrimage there when he was a shepherd at Diego Martin. Other Curepe leaders, including D. and B., overestimated affiliations with their present churches by ten years or more.

All Baptists recognize the importance of credentials and proprietary rights. They also stress that it is easier for a rich man to become a paramount leader than for a poor man, but do not perceive this as a contradiction within the faith. A worthy candidate, they claim, cannot be kept from high church rank by lack of money. On the other hand, they concede that rich members have an easier time advancing.

When members discuss the relationship between wealth and church advancement, they discuss it with reference to other churches, not their own. To admit, for example, that one's paramount leader occupied his position solely because he owned the church would put one's church in an unfavorable light. Also, to admit that wealth plays a part in personal advancement would detract from not only the status of wealthier church members but that of poorer ones as well because everyone pays equally for advancement. Fees for the mourning ceremony vary from church to church, but within the same church all pay the same for the rite.

Baptists do recognize financial mechanisms for church advancement and, even after noting that the rich advance faster, point out that it is God the Father who permits them to have money. Nothing occurs without the Creator's approval; therefore, correlations between wealth and advancement represent the "will of God." Of course, if a rival advances, Baptists are quick to accuse him of simony (purchase of church office).

East Indian Baptists

The comparatively large number of East Indians occupying high positions within the faith provides another illustration of the relationship between wealth and church rank. East Indians, who constitute about 40 percent of the island population, are only a small minority within the faith. Because Baptists see themselves as part of an international religious body, it is not seen as surprising that some East Indians should be accepted into the faith. What is surprising, in light of Baptist racial attitudes, is that so many Indians exercise authority in the highest church councils.

Baptists conceive themselves as part of a universal church. They expect converts of many races and nationalities and believe that it is only natural—in the case of this researcher—that a white man should come from the United States to learn of their religion. Leaders publicly profess that Baptists must convert the whole world and that "God the Father is no respecter of color."

Despite outward professions to the contrary, many Baptists do evidence prejudice against nonblack participants. There is no question in the minds of many members that theirs is a religion for the black man, that they are under no obligation to share their power with the rest of the world, and that black Spiritual Baptists represent the "chosen people."

Spiritual Baptists are willing to bring their message to East Indians, Americans, and Chinese only because other blacks will not listen to them. A frequently cited Biblical justification is found in the Book of Hebrews. When the evangelist Paul took his message to the Hebrews, they would not heed his words; therefore, he took the Gospel to the gentiles. "If the blacks will not heed our message, we will take it to anyone who will listen."

As is apparent from the above, racial attitudes are very complex and, at times, contradictory. It is to be expected that East Indians would experience considerable opposition in the faith. Blacks and East Indians alike have stated that this is the case.

An important factor in East Indian prominence is their relative wealth. There are eight East Indian Baptists in Curepe. All have above-median incomes for the community. All are landowners. The lowest-ranking East Indian is a captain. The highest ranking is a pointer who plans to open his own church.

Racial attitudes sometimes mean that East Indians must mourn more frequently than their black coreligionists. Those interviewed claimed that it takes them more trips to the mourning room to gain ranks equivalent to those of their black brethren. They did not, however, seem to be dissuaded by this. Even though they may advance less during each ceremony, they participate in the rite more often, creating an overall pattern of rapid church advancement. The captain in my study is only twenty-eight years old, while the pointer who aspires to be a paramount leader is only forty-three. Both men are considered young for their respective positions. The former participated in mourning rites twelve times before attaining his present rank; the latter mourned three times a year for five years in a row.

Due in part to racial prejudice, East Indian Baptist leaders experience greater difficulty fulfilling high ranks once they have attained them. Their directives are frequently ignored, attempts to assert authority are thwarted, and they sometimes serve as scapegoats for misfortune within the church. Prejudices are especially strong in those Curepe churches practicing Shango. Members of these churches openly espouse "black pride," claiming that African religions are exclusively for "Africans."

In light of the above, it is interesting that seven out of eight East Indian Baptists were initially attracted to the faith by attendance at Shango feasts. Shango has long held fascination for the East Indian community, possibly because of similarities between African and Hindu rites.[10] For whatever reason, more East Indians are involved in Shango than attend Baptist worship. In 1977, I attended a Shango feast in nearby Tunapuna and noted over twenty East Indians in attendance. East Indians did not become possessed by African spirits, but they did return nightly for the duration of the feast—in this case, four consecutive nights. Such feasts provide ample opportunity for contact between black Baptists and East Indians.

At times, East Indians derive benefits through association with Baptist churches. While they may be victims of prejudice within the faith, fellow Baptists actively support them in conflicts with non-Baptists, including non-Baptist blacks. Merchants are able to attract customers through their Baptist affiliations, since Baptists in Curepe prefer to do business exclusively with other Baptists.

On the other hand, East Indian Baptists often suffer for their faith. Conversion to the Baptist church is not highly regarded within the East Indian community and frequently meets with objections from family, friends, and neighbors. All East Indian Baptists in my sample had a history of family discord prior to joining the faith. Two informants specifically emphasized conflicts with their fathers. One factor that enables East Indian Baptists to devote so much time, energy, and resources to their new religion is that many have severed all family ties.

In church life, East Indians have become most dominant in denominational affairs. If the entire island is considered, East Indian Baptists seem to occupy positions of bishop or archbishop in numbers disproportionate to their total numbers in the faith.

Membership and Recruitment

Baptist leaders claim that church membership has remained stable since the 1950s. Prior to 1953, they add, membership was harder to estimate because the church was illegal and many Baptists had gone "underground." Even today, church records are not always up to date or reliable. Denominational organizations are given primary responsibility for the maintenance of membership statistics, and while many churches do not belong to any denominational organization, other churches belong to more than one. Also, Baptist leaders do not always provide accurate statistics to their denominations. Some leaders inflate the number of members in their churches so as to increase their own influence in denominational affairs.

When churchmen are asked to estimate the number of Baptists on the island, the most frequent response is ten thousand, consisting of one thousand congregations of one hundred members each. Since one hundred members times one thousand churches equals one hundred thousand members and not the reported ten thousand, I do not believe the Baptists meant this estimate to be taken literally. I believe they meant that there are "hundreds of Baptist churches." Moreover, Baptists recognize that some churches have fewer than one hundred members and that some churches have more than two hundred fifty members; nevertheless, it is contended that the figure of ten thousand is essentially an accurate one. Government statistics (official census counts, etc.) do not deal specifically with the religion. Baptists fall within the categories of "Regular Baptists" or "Others" (which includes various Hindu, Islamic, and "African" groups). Many Spiritual Baptists prefer to list themselves as Presbyterians, Methodists, Catholics, or Pentecostals for census purposes.

Many Baptist leaders believe that one hundred is the ideal number of members for a well-functioning church. Twenty-two is the number of leadership positions available within each church, and competition for these positions becomes extremely strong after church membership exceeds one hundred. On the other hand, when there are fewer than one hundred congregants, the pool of available talent is sharply diminished and some individuals must perform multiple church duties.

Actual membership within Curepe churches ranged from 68 to 280. In the first case, the church was very new and held service in the living room of its founder-paramount leader. In the second case, many members expressed dissatisfaction with their church, which they claimed was "too big." Ambitious Baptists complain

Table 3
RELIGIOUS AFFILIATION, TRINIDAD AND TOBAGO, 1970

Religion	Number of Adherents
Anglican	168,521
Baptist (including Spiritual Baptists)	6,774
Church of God	5,050
Hindu	230,209
Methodist	15,507
Moravian	6,527
Muslim	58,271
Presbyterian	39,363
Catholic	331,733
Adventists	16,673
Other	52,443

SOURCE: Republic of Trinidad and Tobago, Population Census Division, Central Statistical Office. *1970 Census Bulletin*, Number 5 (1975).
NOTE: N = 827,957. Many respondents listed more than one affiliation.

that they are not able to advance rapidly in large churches and begin to attend services elsewhere.

Members of large churches do not attend one church regularly but tend to spread their loyalties over several congregations. One large Curepe church (140 members) meets every other week so its members will be able to establish contacts at other churches. This is not seen as a desirable situation, but given slim prospects for advancement within larger churches, it is deemed to be inevitable.

The number of leadership positions within each church is crucial to growth because all major rituals within the faith pertain, either directly or indirectly, to the attainment of higher rank. I have never met a Baptist who was content with his present rank; nor are any provisions made for members of the faith who are basically satisfied with their current status. High rank is *the* reward for loyal church members, and leaders would not know how to control members who were not upwardly mobile.

Recruitment has a high priority within the faith, but Baptists do not appear to be very successful in their attempts to convert

Table 4

MEMBERSHIP PROFILE, MT. TABOR SPIRITUAL BAPTIST CHURCH

Age	Female	Male
10-19	10	8
20-29	10	3
30-39	25	3
40-49	17	2
50-59	15	0
60-69	5	2
70	1	1
Total	83	19

new members, especially when compared with the amount of energy devoted to this activity. Missionary campaigns and street proselytizing, while highly visible, are largely ineffective, and few of my informants admitted to being attracted to the faith by these tactics. Moreover, Baptists are seldom successful in converting their own children to the faith, and church membership rarely follows kinship lines. Only one of Leader D.'s seven children is a practicing Baptist, while Mother R.'s only family convert is a son-in-law who was already a practicing Baptist before marrying her daughter. She persuaded him to stop worshipping at his church of origin, which is about seventy miles away, and to transfer to her church. One way in which Baptists are coping with this is by baptizing children at a younger age. In 1982, I attended a baptism ceremony at Todd's Road, where four out of the five candidates were under fifteen years of age. The leader at Todd's Road claimed that he was "making an experiment" to attract new members and acknowledged that such a thing would not have occurred several years ago. Thus far, the baptism of youths seems restricted to this church and is very controversial.

In other Caribbean religions, such as Shango and Rada, membership in the group often does follow kinship lines. Possessing spirits in Rada,[11] for example, frequently pass from mother to daughter or, more commonly, from grandmother to granddaughter. In the Baptist faith, God the Father, God the Son, and

Table 5

RELIGIONS OF SPIRITUAL BAPTIST LEADERS PRIOR TO JOINING THE
BAPTIST FAITH

Religion	Male	Female
Anglican	2	2
Baptist (London)	1	0
Jehova Witness	1	1
Methodist	2	1
Pentecostal	3	1
Catholic	4	3
Adventist	3	1
Hindu	2	0
No religion	1	0

NOTE: N = 28 Spiritual Baptist leaders, Curepe and vicinity.

God the Holy Ghost are equally accessible to all, and there are
no inherited powers to be passed to the next generation.

Baptists make few provisions for the religious socialization of
children. Leaders contend that the Baptist faith is a religion for
adults, and they refuse to sponsor programs of religious education and/or Sunday School. No leader would consider baptizing a child who was not at least twelve years old. Some children,
however, do experience minimal early exposure to the religion.
Women frequently bring their young children to church with
them because they do not wish to leave them home alone.

A general lack of concern for socialization in the faith may, as
Troeltsch and Weber posited, have far-reaching consequences
for church organization. As Niebuhr noted, "By its very nature
the sectarian type of organization is valid for one generation.
The children born to the voluntary members of the first generation began to make a sect a church long before they have arrived
at the years of discretion. For with their coming the sect must
take on the character of an educational and disciplinary institution, with the purpose of bringing the new generation into
conformity with ideals and customs which have become traditional. Rarely does a second generation hold the convictions it
has inherited with a fervor equal to that of its fathers."[12] Since
there are so few second-generation Baptists, the transition from
sectarian to church-like organization is never completed.

Although kinship ties are not a strong predictor of church affiliation among the Baptists, the church does advocate strong family and kinship ties. Leaders preach against divorce, "friending,"[13] and desertion, and admonish Baptist males not to "play around" with many women. Baptist males are expected to have one wife only. It does not appear to matter greatly whether a couple is legally married. It is most important for a man to remain faithful to one woman and her children.

Marriages between Baptists and non-Baptists are especially volatile, and much marital discord can be attributed directly to the church. Mourning ceremonies, pilgrimage tickets, assessments, and other Baptist fund-raising activities make heavy demands on family budgets. Non-Baptist mates frequently resent money given to the church. Members are counseled to convert their wayward spouses, but under no circumstances are they encouraged to leave them. It is nobler, in the eyes of a believer, to suffer for one's faith, and many women provide long testimonies of their martyrdom at the hands of unsympathetic spouses.

Simpson characterized the Baptists as a "lower-class" religion.[14] Although many, particularly older, Baptists have remained poor, many more "middle-class" and "upper-middle-class" individuals have joined the faith in recent years. One measure of economic advancement is the growing number of church members who own automobiles.

Baptist values are not at all antithetical to economic advancement. Leaders admonish their followers to work hard and be frugal, values frequently associated with the Protestant ethic. Moreover, many leaders are able to assist members of their congregation in obtaining jobs. Petty entrepreneurs, such as Leader D., hire only fellow Baptists; and even non-Baptist employers, such as the owner of the Curepe woolens mill, ask Baptist leaders to recommend individuals for possible employment. The woolens mill owner believes that Baptists are reliable workers.

I. M. Lewis has suggested that many Caribbean religions exist primarily to enhance the status of their participants.[15] Many others have also noted that Caribbean religions provide the individual with "another system of prestige."[16] According to Mischel, this is a major function of the Shango cult in Trinidad; that is, through possession by African deities, individuals are able to act out powerful superior roles that she contends are denied to them in Trinidadian society.[17]

This does appear to be a primary function of the Spiritual Baptist church in Trinidad. Through the mourning ceremony, individuals are able to attain ranks higher than similar positions of authority that would be available to them in the outside world. On the other hand, many wealthy Baptists who already are powerful members of the community, also mourn. They also use the Baptist religion to enhance their status.

I do not feel that enhancement of status is unique to the Caribbean. All religious groups seem to have the potential to enhance the status of their members; for example, in the United States a man who is not able to become president of his company may obtain satisfaction by becoming the chairman of the board of deacons at his church. This does not mean that he wanted to become the chairman of the board of deacons because he was "deprived." Had he become president of his company, he may have continued his struggle for a position on the board of deacons. The problem of status enhancement and religion is much more complex than Lewis and Mischel have described it.

The Spiritual Baptist church is not what Lanternari would term a "religion of the oppressed."[18] There are poor Baptists, but in many cases these Baptists are poor because they are old and live on a government pension, about $60TT a month, and they cannot find part-time work to supplement their incomes. Leaders claim that their churches "contains rich and poor peoples alike" and that God the Father does not distinguish between the rich man and the poor man. In practice, wealthier members do enjoy distinct advantages in the faith.

Many occupations are represented in the Baptist church. Some members are unemployed, some members are domestics, some members are petty entrepreneurs, and some members are schoolteachers, bureaucrats, writers, and politicians. One of the most successful Baptist leaders on the island is the doorman at the Hilton Hotel in Port of Spain. Nine Curepe Baptists attended university, and one Baptist who has a master's degree in psychology is preparing a book on Jungian symbolism in Baptist ritual.

All Curepe informants claim to have been attracted originally to the church by vaguely perceived personal problems. Many reported a general feeling of malaise, a lack of energy, a sense that their lives had become meaningless. Conversion accounts stressed drowsiness, lack of friends, depression, family problems, and job dissatisfaction prior to joining the faith. From this, one aspect of conversion is very clear. It is not, by most accounts, the church that converts the Baptist, but the Baptist who seeks conversion.

Baptists believe that many personal problems stem from being at the wrong level or rank within the religion. Each of the twenty-two ranks listed previously is associated with specific duties, and the relationship between specific duties and church rank is fairly rigid. On the other hand, with the exception of the four top ranks (warrior, commander, inspector, and judge) and the bottom two ranks (brother and sister), each informant provided a slightly different variant of the chain of command (see Table 2), and male and female versions of the chain of command almost always differed.

In Moruga, church ranks are gender specific; women mourn to become nurses, teachers, and mothers, while men mourn to become captains, shepherds, and leaders.[19] In other churches, however, I encountered male nurses and teachers, and one female shepherd. Ranks such as prover, diver, star-gazer, or surveyor are not gender specific.

As noted, each church has one paramount leader (usually a male). In addition, each church has a paramount mother who enjoys a slightly different status than do all other mothers. The paramount mother may be the mother who has worked with the paramount leader the longest, the most senior church mother, or—most frequently—the wife of the paramount leader.

Because many Baptist women occupy the position of paramount mother solely on the basis of marriage, it is very difficult for them to maintain this position after their husbands die. Between 1979 and 1982, two paramount leaders (males) died in Curepe; in both cases, their wives had served as paramount mothers in their respective churches. When I returned in 1982, I found that one woman—whose husband had owned the church building outright—had retained her position, while the other woman—whose husband had led the church on the basis of his "credentials"—lost her position to the wife of the new paramount leader.

Most male paramount leaders stated that they prefer to have their own wives as paramount mothers because "things is easier that way." Ambitious Baptist women prefer to attend the churches of unmarried leaders, where, they believe, they can become a paramount mother according to their "merits." In most cases, it is the paramount leader who decides, although in one prominent Port of Spain church, the paramount mother is always the most senior mother irrespective of the paramount leader's preference. This particular church is also the headquarters for one of the largest Spiritual Baptist "denominations," and the position of paramount leader is hotly contested. Members found that it usually takes several years to find a new paramount leader and decided that it would be best not to be without both a paramount leader and a paramount mother for such a prolonged period.

Bastide claims that New World blacks have a "passion" for titles and that "one gets the impression that the complex hierarchy has little to do with the actual work that is carried out."[20] This is not true in the Baptist religion, however, because hierarchy and rank do relate directly to the division of labor within the church.

Baptists must perform duties associated with their ranks and, more important, duties associated with all other ranks conceived of as lower in the church hierarchy. The implications of such an arrangement are far reaching. If captains conceive of themselves as having obtained a higher rank than that of a preacher, for example, captains not only begin service and maintain the church but interpret scripture as well. If, on the other hand, captains consider themselves inferior to preachers, they may begin service but must defer to preachers in matters of interpretation.

This leads to confusion. In one Curepe church, preachers did believe themselves superior to captains, while captains refused to acknowledge preachers' authority over them. This gave rise to heated debate among not only members of these respective ranks but also other church members who had their own ideas about how things should be run.

There are, however, advantages to this loose system. Since Baptist ranks are like Chinese nesting boxes—each rank contains the duties of all lower ranks—it is possible for a church to function with very few members. A leader and his wife, for example, could perform all duties necessary to run a church. This is frequently the case when a new church is founded.

Denominational Organizations

Curepe Baptists recognize four competing denominational organizations on the island: (1) the National Evangelical Spiritual Baptist Faith Archdiocese, under the leadership of Archbishop B., which claims to be affiliated with A.M.E. Zion Church in Africa and some Rastafarian groups in Jamaica; (2) the National Ecclesiastical Council of Churches Spiritual Baptist of Trinidad and Tobago, Inc.; (3) the West Indian United Sacred Order of Spiritual Baptist Churches, Inc., under Bishop C.; and (4) the Ambassadors for Christ Spiritual Baptist, Ltd., under Pastor D.[21] As these titles imply, all denominational organizations in Trinidad have international pretensions, although to my knowledge no organization listed above has an international membership.

Each denomination is autonomous, and churches appear to join and leave these organizations without respect to doctrinal differences or similarities. Leader D.'s church once joined the National Evangelical Spiritual Baptist Faith Archdiocese, even though he does not believe that the A.M.E. Zion Church or Rastafarianism are compatible with the Baptist faith. Moreover, many island churches belong to more than one denomination, while other churches eschew denominational ties entirely.

Denominations license leaders to perform marriage ceremonies, aid in fund raising, and contribute monies toward the defense of Baptist leaders accused of capital crimes. Toward the defense of leaders, two denominations (the National Ecclesiastical Council of Churches Spiritual Baptist and the West Indian United Sacred Order of Spiritual Baptist Churches) retain Port of Spain lawyers. The denominations also provide ambitious leaders with opportunities to attain higher ranks, such as bishop and archbishop.

Church-state relations are extremely complex throughout the

Caribbean, and the Baptist case is further complicated by the alleged Baptist affiliation of the former prime minister, Eric Williams. Government officials are careful not to give preferential treatment to any religion, yet no government prosecutor wishes to antagonize members of a religious group that has especially been encouraged by the PNM.[22]

A major area of legal contention centers on performance of mourning rites. The state argues that Baptist leaders should be held responsible for the physical well-being of mourners. Mourning rites are believed to have curative powers, and because so many participants enter the rite in an unhealthy state, every two or three years someone dies during the ordeal, resulting in a government inquiry. Government prosecutors assert that poor diet and damp conditions in the mourning room are contributing factors to mourners' deaths. Leaders, they contend, must refuse to mourn individual candidates too weak to withstand the rigors of the ceremony.

Leaders defend themselves in such cases by claiming that they take every possible precaution to insure the mourners' survival. This is very difficult to prove, and leaders interpret government charges as evidence for government persecution. They claim that someone in "high places" is trying to discredit them.

It is unclear exactly how much support denominational organizations are able to provide in these circumstances. While some do make provisions for legal defense and provide testimonies in court on a leader's behalf, few cases ever reach that level. Lawyers retained by the organizations are paid small retainers of $30-50TT per year and are most interested in constitutional matters raised by government charges. Intradenominational relations are highly politicized. Formal statements of support cannot usually be expected because, in most cases, one leader's problems can be turned to a rival's advantage. If a leader is preoccupied with legal matters, he is said to have less time to devote to denominational and church affairs; in short, he is very vulnerable.

Denominational organizations are no more effective in other areas of church life. In the past it has proved difficult to reach agreement as to the importance of a particular missionary venture. Missions are, for the most part, projects undertaken by individual leaders who believe, or profess to believe, that they are working in the name of the organization. Between 1974 and 1978, all Venezuelan missionary campaigns were sponsored by individual congregations, and each congregation worked independently of the others.

Leaders state that as far as they are concerned the major function of denominational organizations is to provide them with ranks of bishop and archbishop. There are thirty-five openings in all. Each denomination has eight bishops and—with the exception of the national evangelical organization, whose archbishop serves a life term—each denominational organization also has one archbishop who serves a one-year term. If a man is elected a bishop in one organization, this does not preclude his becoming a candidate for archbishop in another organization. Also, it is possible, although very rare, to become an archbishop without having first served as a bishop.

There is much interdenominational switching as leaders attempt to maximize their chances of becoming bishops or archbishops. One Curepe leader joined three denominations over a two-year period in his efforts to become an archbishop—thus far without success.

Denominational ties are fragile as churches join and drop out of these organizations to suit leadership objectives. Accurate records of denominational affiliation are often unavailable, and individual church members frequently do not know their church's current affiliation, if any.

Anthropologists have postulated that higher levels of organization may give rise to homogenization of social groups.[23] In the Baptist case, this does not seem to have occurred because: (1) denominational organizations lack centralized authority and funding to exercise control over member congregations. Nominal dues of $10TT ($6US) per year are assessed, but denominations have no way of collecting them. Moreover, records are not kept as to which congregations have actually paid their dues. And (2) denominational organizations serve as extensions of individual ambition rather than as a focus for collective loyalty. Leaders use them primarily as means to an end—in most cases, attainment of a bishopric. These factors combine to produce a higher level of organization, which fosters diversity rather than unity within the religion.

Church-State Relations

One difficulty in the classification of the Baptist faith as a "church" may be that individual Baptist churches vary considerably in their attitudes toward major institutions in Trinidadian society. Some church leaders, for example, actively support the government, while other church leaders claim that the Baptists are constantly persecuted by the government. Those leaders who claim to be persecuted make much of a 1917 ordinance introduced in the Legislative Council to ban the faith:

A condition of affairs has arisen in the colony by reason of the practice of the sect or body calling itself the Shouters which has, as far as the government sees, made it necessary to come to this house and submit proposals for the interference in the practice of that body. Apparently the Shouters have had a somewhat stormy history from all I have been able to learn regarding them. They seem, if they did not rise there, to have flourished exceedingly in St. Vincent, and to have made of themselves such an unmitigated nuisance that they had to be legislated out of existence. They then came to Trinidad and continual complaints have been received by the Government from that time on as to their practices.[24]

Leaders who support the government admit that the faith was officially banned between 1917 and 1953 but stress that the ordinance was never strictly enforced and that the ban did little to slow the spread of the Baptist religion. The church at Belmont, the alleged subject of the original ordinance, continued to hold weekly services without interruption between 1917 and 1953. Also, several Baptist leaders assert that the government did not close a single church between 1917 and 1953; nor were any Baptist leaders imprisoned during that period. Some leaders, they claim, like to exaggerate the degree of government persecution because there is prestige associated with martyrdom within the faith. They also claim that the real purpose of the ordinance was not to curtail the Baptist religion but to curtail noise at Baptist services.

Herskovits and Herskovits, however, reported very strained

relations between Baptist churches and the government. In 1939 two separate charges against Shouters groups were lodged, and convictions were obtained. The government fined the head of the group and the man on whose land the meeting had been held.[25] According to Archbishop G., fines were also imposed in 1940, 1941, and 1945.

Herskovits suggests that the religion was banned primarily because "more conventional denominations wanted to counteract the inroads these 'shouters' were making into their following,"[26] and in 1952 he testified in front of the Legislative Assembly in favor of revoking the government ban on the religion. For this service, many Spiritual Baptist leaders remember Herskovits with fondness.

There is no evidence that the Baptists were making inroads among members of conventional denominations at the turn of this century. I believe that the reason the faith was banned was primarily because services were noisy and held in crowded residential areas.[27] If services in 1917 were as loud as unamplified services in 1978, Belmont residents had good reason to complain. Walls are thin, housing is cramped, and the sound of Baptist worship reverberates throughout the neighborhood.

Also, in reference to the ordinance, it must be noted again that there is little reason to believe that Baptists moved from St. Vincent to avoid persecution. Many Vincentians moved to Trinidad long after the Trinidad ordinance was passed. Chief incentives for my informants were overwhelmingly economic—they said that there were many more opportunities for employment in Trinidad—and the Vincentian ban, which was passed five years before the Trinidad ban, was no stricter nor more effective against the spread of the faith there than was the Trinidad ban.

5 • Leadership Decisions and Church Economics

ECONOMICALLY, each Spiritual Baptist church is completely independent. All monies taken in are essentially managed by the paramount leader, although other high-ranking church members may be consulted before major expenditures are made. In all cases, the paramount leader is solely responsible for the economic well-being of his church, and his reputation as a successful leader is closely tied to his ability to raise funds and spend them wisely for the benefit of the group.

Baptist leaders have mixed feelings about economics. Many claim that they are not at all interested in money, buildings, or property—but that such things are seen as the measures of "success." They do participate in the competitive capitalist economy of the nation, and they do tend to rank one another on the basis of acquisitions.

Baptist church expenditures are of two types: (1) those directly associated with ritual activities and the physical maintenance of the church, and (2) "luxuries" and/or items less vital for day-to-day church operations. All leaders in my sample involve their churches in both types of expenditures. Luxury spending is essential because it provides a means of "testing" one's leadership potential. Leaders who do not participate in luxury spending may lose their authority base within the church.

Chief fund-raising activities include free-will offerings, missions, and pilgrimages. Free-will offerings, consisting of contributions collected during worship and personal solicitations, are a constant source of financial support. Offerings during worship are small, ranging from $5 to $10TT per week, and many prefer to donate their time instead of cash. Still others prefer to make their offerings "in kind" (a candle, a sheet of tin, a loaf of bread, etc.).

Church members are expected to tithe, that is, to give 10 percent of all earnings to the church; however, few meet this expectation. Some feel that 10 percent is excessive, while others suggest that they would be quite willing to give more money to the work of their church but cannot afford to do so. Inflation is high in Trinidad, and extra money goes toward the purchase of durable goods and canned foods. Members believe that these goods will rise in price.

Leaders, within the context of the pulpit and in private consultations, admonish members to tithe, but they have no way of forcing members to contribute. Leaders are not supposed to be overly concerned with money and should not, it is believed, keep track of individual giving. Baptists state that an individual's gifts to the church are largely matters between him or herself and God, in this case God the Father, who is not easily swayed by offerings. Also, patterns of church assessment in emergencies militate against the principle of tithing. Members, in times of trouble, are asked to contribute equal shares to the project at hand rather than divide expenses proportionately according to wealth. If new galvanize is needed for the church roof, for example, the cost is divided equally among members. The rich and the poor share alike in the financial burden.

Very little money is available through assessment because donations are keyed to the poorest members of the congregations. If leaders were forced to make church improvements by assessments or offerings, church buildings would deteriorate. Only one piece of tin could be purchased at a time; or as is sometimes the case, leaders would be forced to buy half-sheets and scraps to cover gaping holes and rust spots.

In newer churches, assessments and free-will offerings are often inadequate to meet basic expenses. Ritual paraphernalia (bells, flower pots, and urns) may be borrowed or rented from neighboring churches. Borrowing occurs among Baptists,

Pentecostals, Catholics, and various other groups on the island and need not stay within denominational groups. In extremely poor churches, services are curtailed—either shortened or held once every two or three weeks—in order to conserve candles and incense. In some Curepe churches, weekly offerings do not even meet the cost of candles. Between fourteen and twenty candles are burned in a two-hour service. Baptists prefer twelve-inch white tapered candles imported from the United States and Canada that cost about fifty cents each. A two-hour service, therefore, costs seven dollars in candles alone. As mentioned previously, many services last longer than two hours, and total offerings are often less than seven dollars.

Fund-raising Activities

To compensate for shortfalls in church income, a number of fund-raising activities are used. Street proselytizing and/or local missions are one way to add to church coffers, albeit not a particularly lucrative one. On any Friday or Saturday night it seems as if almost every street corner in Trinidad has a Spiritual Baptist "on mission."[1] Some Baptists travel in groups, while others prefer to proselytize alone. In either case, few collect much more than enough for bus fare home, and no one seems to believe that proselytizing is an effective fund-raising activity. Nevertheless, it is a prevalent fund-raising activity and is undertaken by most Baptists at some time during their religious careers.

The number of Baptists who claim to have been attracted to the faith by street proselytizing is negligible, and even staunch supporters of the technique admit that it may repel as many potential converts as it tends to attract. It is widely agreed that street proselytizing does little to improve the "image" of the faith.

Despite these drawbacks, Baptists persist in their missions because they believe that it is good for members to speak publicly for their faith. If missions do not make a great deal of money, at least they do not lose any money. If missions do not have much of an impact on the outside world, at least they may strengthen the Baptist's perception of himself and his role in the religion. Also, missionizing is one of the few activities engaged in by all members of the congregation without respect to rank. Every Baptist can go on mission.

Pilgrimages, by far the most complex and lucrative of fundraising activities, provide Baptists with most of their income. A pilgrimage is a joint worship service involving two or more churches. These churches are usually located some distance from one another, and church members raise money by selling bus tickets to these services. What follows is a description of a typical pilgrimage in Trinidad. (I was unable to attend any extended pilgrimages to Tobago or St. Vincent, so I am not able to provide much detail concerning such pilgrimages. I assume that they are similar.)

A typical pilgrimage lasts one day only. Early in the morning, all who have purchased tickets meet at the sponsoring church and board buses. Once the buses are moving, Baptists begin singing, clapping, and—sometimes—dancing in the aisles. At times, high-ranking church members interrupt to make announcements or to offer prayer. The paramount leader, who is the organizer of the pilgrimage, should not take an active part in the singing and celebration. His duty, according to informants, is to "pray for a successful journey."

When the destination has been reached—usually in one or two hours—Baptists leave their buses and congregate outside the host church, whose members also remain outside until after a ritual of "greeting" has been completed. In rituals of greeting, both hosts and guests line up behind their respective paramount leaders, and two shepherds and two teachers from each church raise shepherd's crooks in the form of twin arches in front of the church entrance (see Photograph 1). The two paramount leaders face each other, then put their heads to each other's shoulders—left to right to left. The visiting leader enters the church, followed by his congregation and then by members of the host congregation. The paramount leader of the host church is always the last to enter.

After everyone is seated in the church, the host leader rises, offers a short homily, and "turns over" his church to the visiting leader. From that time on, the visiting leader is—at least theoretically—in charge of the service. In practice, however, visiting leaders rarely exercise authority during these ceremonies, and no one seriously believes that a paramount leader would ever relinquish power in his own church.[2]

Services continue for about two hours, there is a break for lunch,[3] succeeded by two or three more hours of ritual. Buses depart in the late afternoon in order to return to the sponsoring church by evening. There is some singing and clapping on the return trip, but usually the return trip is much quieter than the outward journey.

Sponsoring churches incur some risks and reap great profits from this activity. They must provide capital for chartering buses, printing tickets, and making final arrangements at distant churches. In return, they are entitled to all profits from ticket sales and half of all offerings collected during the service. In all, sponsors risk one or two hundred dollars in order to gain two or three hundred dollars. It is possible to earn more than 100 percent profit.

Lesser benefits accrue to host churches. They must make preparations to receive their guests ("spruce up the church," etc.), clean up after service, and stand to gain only half the offering in payment for their inconvenience. There is some prestige associated with being chosen as a pilgrimage site, but the benefits to hosts are neither as patent nor as direct as benefits that accrue to sponsoring churches.

Host churches, by and large, are chosen for their inaccessibility to the sponsoring church. Sponsors seek sites not easily visited by church members, and their ultimate goal, rarely attained, is to sponsor a pilgrimage to a church that no one in their congregation has been to before. Also, pilgrimages to distant churches are more profitable for their promoters because bus charters are based on a flat daily rate, whereas pilgrimage tickets are priced according to the distance traveled. It costs a promoter no more to travel ten miles than it costs him to travel thirty miles, but he is able to charge more for tickets to a distant site. Some leaders, nevertheless, do sponsor pilgrimages to neighboring churches. In such cases, they usually sponsor side trips to Maracas Bay or Manzanilla and are able to charge additional money.

Distant churches are most desirable as pilgrimage sites for another reason. Leaders constantly compete with one another for followers, with the most intense competition between leaders of neighboring churches. If it can be avoided, leaders would prefer not to allow their followers to have too much contact with area rivals. Distant churches pose less of a threat in that regard. In most cases, it would be impractical for members of the sponsoring church to commute so far to regular worship. Leaders, thus, do not have to be overly concerned about leaders within the host church "convicting" and/or stealing their followers.

Distances in Trinidad are social as well as geographical categories and cannot be measured solely by the mile. Towns that may, in fact, appear close on the map may be considered "distant" because they are inaccessible; that is, they are not on jitney cab and bus routes. Toco, although it is only about thirty miles from Curepe, is considered "distant" because it is difficult to get to, requiring three transfers by jitney cab and two transfers by public bus. Without a private car, it is considered a whole day's trip to get to Toco on a Sunday (when public transportation runs less frequently), and therefore churches in Toco are desirable pilgrimage sites. On the other hand, Point Fortin, which is farther away from Curepe in terms of miles, is considered "too close" because it is on major bus routes and transportation is easily arranged. Leaders do sponsor pilgrimages to Point Fortin, but include side trips to the pitch lake, Mayoro Beach, or Siparia, where a famous shrine is located.

The case of Point Fortin serves to illustrate other factors that may come into play in choosing a pilgrimage site. Point Fortin's location, close to several oil wells and refineries, has resulted in economic advancement for people and churches in the area. Unemployment in Point Fortin is much lower than that of the Northwest, and, by and large, area wages are much higher. Church contributions are more generous in the area, and some leaders do not have to rely on pilgrimages to meet operating expenses. Southern churches sponsor pilgrimages less often than their northwestern brethren, and because of this are considered more desirable as hosts.[4] They can be visited without as much risk of reciprocation. Also, southern churches tend to be the most elaborate Baptist churches on the island. They are large, well built, architecturally interesting—in short, suitable sites for joint worship.

Regional variations in religious life serve to demonstrate that the pilgrimage is not endemic to the religion but has been developed in certain areas to meet specific needs. Henney records no cases of pilgrimage behavior among the Baptists of St. Vincent,[5] and Angelina Pollak-Eltz does not mention them in regard to the Baptists of Grenada.[6] Pilgrimages, it seems, are a unique response to conditions prevailing in Trinidad. My data indicate that when a church is able to function without pilgrimages, leaders cease to sponsor them.[7] Even in the Northwest, very wealthy and established churches sponsor fewer pilgrimages.

The history of the pilgrimage as an institution is unclear. Older informants were unable to remember churches without pilgrimages, and no one was able to recollect exactly when the pilgrimage as an institution began. Informants do remember, however, the first time that they personally attended or sponsored a pilgrimage, and they contend that there were fewer pilgrimages in the early decades of this century than there are at present.

As mentioned previously, it is better, from a financial point of view, to sponsor a pilgrimage than to host one. According to Baptist etiquette, there is little a host church can do to avoid becoming a pilgrimage site. Sponsoring churches send a delegate, usually a lower-ranking member, to announce the pilgrimage at the host church. These announcements are made toward the end of service and are followed by a period of mandatory silence. There is, therefore, no opportunity for churches to decline host duties. Guests, in effect, invite themselves.

Few excuses are acceptable to decline host duties. Even if two churches are coming on the same day, arrangements are made so that both visiting churches may worship together; or one church comes in the morning, and the other comes in the afternoon. Mourning ceremonies, weddings, baptisms, and other church rites must be rescheduled so as to accommodate sponsoring churches. In some cases even funerals must be rescheduled.

With so little choice, there is usually some resentment among members of the host church. Like all uninvited guests, pilgrims may appear disruptive, messy, and demanding. In pilgrimages attended by the author, it was apparent that pilgrims, because they had paid for their tickets, considered themselves paying guests and felt it was the host church's responsibility to serve them. It is of interest, in light of the above, that many churches have not withdrawn from the pilgrimage circuit entirely. To my knowledge, no Baptist church has ever refused a pilgrimage, nor are there institutionalized mechanisms for declining pilgrimages within the faith.

Church leaders, I believe, tolerate pilgrimages because they are seen as part of a general network of reciprocity. Most leaders recognize that their own financial position is very dependent on their ability to raise funds in this manner. Pilgrimages may serve as a final line of defense against insolvency. Successful pilgrimages constitute one alternative to closing a church; and even the most prestigious churches are vulnerable because, as will be demonstrated, they, too, are compelled to overextend themselves. While some leaders are said to abuse pilgrimage privileges, potential benefits to be derived from the institution far outweigh its potential for inconvenience and abuse.[8]

While cooperation from host churches is necessary for a successful pilgrimage, fund raising takes place primarily within the sponsoring church. It is very much a self-contained, "bootstrap" operation. Church members purchase tickets from their own leaders to demonstrate support for their church. In a highly successful pilgrimage, nearly all church members purchase at least one ticket, with more ambitious members expected to buy three or four. In the unlikely event that a church fails to make money on a pilgrimage, it is said to indicate general dissatisfaction among church members. I was told that this never happened in Curepe.

In 1976 and 1977, pilgrimage tickets sold for between four and six dollars apiece, payable in advance. In 1978, several churches began charging nine and ten dollars for their tickets. Many Baptists felt this was excessive. It is still possible, they contended, to make money on four-dollar pilgrimages. By 1982, however, most pilgrimage tickets sold for eight to twelve dollars apiece.

The degree of advance planning necessary for a successful pilgrimage venture belies local assertions that Spiritual Baptist leaders are incapable of rational economic action. All aspects of pilgrimage behavior are calculated months before the activity itself takes place. Tickets are professionally printed at least three months in advance, and many leaders will not charter a bus before enough tickets have been presold to break even. Pilgrimages may be cancelled at any time prior to departure, and refunds must be specifically requested. Loyal church members are not expected to request a refund in these circumstances; therefore, leaders usually obtain enough money to pay printing costs, even when the pilgrimage does not take place.

Leaders have developed a marketing plan that enables them to save face when a pilgrimage does not materialize. Tickets are made available first to church members and only later to other Baptists. Last of all, they are sold to the general public. If an outsider is offered a ticket, chances are good that the pilgrimage will in fact occur.

Host churches, in all cases, are among the last to find out about proposed pilgrimages, although many do learn about a planned pilgrimage before formal announcement is made. At any time before the formal announcement, sponsoring churches may deny (as rumor) assertions that a pilgrimage is being planned. In general, host churches receive about two weeks' notice prior to the arrival of the pilgrims. By that time, accounts are settled with the charter company, usually a government agency, and profits are in the bank.

Sometimes, because paramount leaders themselves do not always visit host churches in advance, pilgrimage tickets are printed for destinations that no longer exist. In 1977, I was sold a ticket to a church in Rio Claro that had folded three years earlier. The pilgrimage site was simply changed to another church in the same area, and pilgrims were not forewarned of the change in itinerary. Leaders contend that pilgrimage destinations should not be important to loyal church members. Opportunities for fellowship and worship far transcend the importance of the site.

Good sites, however, attract outsiders, and outsiders make the difference between a moderately successful and a phenomenally successful pilgrimage. All tickets to outsiders are sold after basic expenses have been met; thus, these sales represent pure profits to their promoters. Exotic destinations are advantageous in selling to outsiders and, sometimes, provide outstanding travel bargains. In 1966, Leader R. sponsored a pilgrimage to St. Vincent, chartering a government boat and selling tickets throughout the Curepe community and at Woodford Square in Port of

Spain. His tickets, while not offering the most luxurious of accommodations for the overnight journey, were 30 percent less than the prevailing fares to the island, and he claims that many non-Baptists took advantage of this. In 1978, I was offered a pilgrimage ticket to Manzanilla for five dollars, about fifty cents less than the jitney cab fare.

There are limits to the number of pilgrimages that can be sponsored by any church over a one-year period. Curepe leaders claim that many members cannot afford to buy more than three tickets per year and that even three tickets may constitute a financial sacrifice for some members. For the years 1976-1978, Curepe churches, on the average, sponsored three pilgrimages and hosted two pilgrimages. One leader attempted to sponsor a fourth pilgrimage in 1976, but it was poorly attended and caused considerable dissension within his church.

Expenditures

Many Baptists claim that a good leader should be able to meet all church expenses without recourse to pilgrimages or assessments. In practice, no leader in the community has tried to accomplish this, and all of them sponsor pilgrimages and demand assessments on a regular basis. Moreover, leaders also use pilgrimages and assessments to obtain certain "luxuries" not included in their regular operating budgets, such as: ritual paraphernalia, microphones, amplifiers, speakers, telephones, electrical power hookups (mainly to power the sound system), embossed stationery, annual dues to denominational organizations, and extensive foreign missionary campaigns. None of the above, as will be demonstrated, is essential for day-to-day church operations.

Case Study I. Mt. C. Spiritual Baptist Church, July 1976

Using a wealthy church member as a reference, Leader W. purchased an expensive sound system for use in his church. He arranged to make payments on the installment plan. The church, however, was unable to make two payments in a row and the system was repossessed. Brother B., a rival of W., pointed out that the church had invested money (the down payment was several hundred dollars) and now had nothing to show for it. This did not bother Leader W., who, two months later, established credit at another store and purchased another sound system (not as elaborate as the first) on time payments. Several church members were upset by this and began attending service elsewhere. Brother B., for example, moved to a church in Las Lomas. Ironically, later that summer Brother B.'s new church voted to buy a set of speakers at B's urgings and these were subsequently repossessed.

Case Study II. Mt. T. Spiritual Baptist Church, 1976

Leader D. had a telephone installed in his church. The congregation was unable to raise money to pay monthly service charges. Rather than have the telephone taken out, D. has the phone "temporarily" disconnected; then as soon as he feels his church can afford it, he has service restored. The leader admits that between 1974 and 1976, the church has not had telephone service for more than a total of three consecutive months.

Neither telephone service nor sound systems are essential for Baptist rituals. Churches are small and sermon delivery dynamic enough so that no one, given normal hearing, would experience difficulty in understanding what is being said. Hymns are rendered with great enthusiasm and at high volume (so high that this is one reason the Baptists are known as "Shouters"). Given the normally high volume of services, an amplification system is redundant at best.

Telephone service is also unnecessary and seldom used. Important messages, including all church communications, must be conveyed by messenger. Children are widely used as message carriers, and, for many Baptists, the act of "sending a messenger" constitutes part of the dramatic structure of an event. Use of messengers signifies the importance of the sender as well as that of the recipient. It implies that the recipient is either too powerful, busy, or inaccessible to deal with directly, and also makes it clear that the sender is too important or busy to go himself. A telephone call, on the other hand, is thought to be demeaning in a religious context. It indicates a lack of respect for the recipient and results in a loss of respect to both parties.

Messengers occupy an important place in Baptist thought. References to messengers in the Bible are cited frequently in sermons and in mourner's tracts. It is believed, as stated previously, that God the Father does not speak directly to man, but through God the Son, God the Holy Ghost, or angels. In the spirit world, powerful beings do not communicate with one another directly but through intermediaries. The world of the spirits, in this case, should be replicated in the world of men.

Telephones may not be utilized for official church business between leaders. Pilgrimages and other affairs must be arranged by personal visitation. Use of the telephone within the church is limited to personal calls, and since few members have home telephones, they make little use of telephone service. In Curepe churches, telephone service appears as what Veblen has labeled a "conspicuous display of consumption."[9] It is used to demonstrate that the church and its leadership are successful in an idiom that all can understand. Since telephone service is supplied and regulated by the government, charges for installation, reinstatement, and monthly service fees are matters of public record. Everyone knows how much telephone service costs.

Church leaders are judged on the basis of their expenditures and are expected to build prosperous-looking churches. It must also be recognized that each time a pastor overspends (at least from the standpoint of rational capitalist economic theory), he "tests" his church. Baptist ideology stresses that churches prosper not because members are careful with their investments (although some leaders do invest in the stock market and government bonds), but because members have found favor with the Lord. Leaders take risks, such as ordering luxuries they cannot possibly pay for in order to prove to themselves and to others that they are following the will of God the Father. In the first case study, while many members became disgruntled over Leader W.'s spending, others pointed out that their sound system was repossessed not because Leader W. had overextended church resources, but because God did not want them to have a sound system at that time. When Leader W. finally did pay for the sound system, members unanimously proclaimed that he was a "great leader" who had "built" the church.

Because church spending is seen as something of a test, leaders are sometimes able to transfer blame for unsuccessful ventures onto other, usually nonpracticing or former, church members. When the congregation is unable to pay its monthly telephone bill, this is taken as a sign from God. It is a time for the congregation to reassess prior actions and look for behavior that may have earned God's disfavor. Any individual who has "fallen" (not lived up to his commitment within the faith) is seen as a potential cause of the problem. To compensate for this, each member is asked to reaffirm publicly his commitment to the church and its leader. A new consensus and, in many cases, a stronger church are the result.

For a variety of reasons, it is often advantageous for church leaders to overspend on luxury items and to promote crises within their churches. It is a "can't lose" situation. If a leader overspends and everything works out, he demonstrates his superior leadership ability; on the other hand, if he overspends and things do not work out, he is able to shift the blame to others in the congregation. Overspending serves to galvanize support and opinion within the church and also provides an opportunity for leaders to discredit rivals and their grievances. It is easier to deal with grievances directly, through accusations of "bad faith," than to contend with gossip spreading through the congregation and potentially undermining support. As in the case of Brother B., disruptive members may leave the church, thus making it easier for leaders to build a new consensus.

Seen from the standpoint of church leadership, overspending on luxury goods is not irrational behavior. It is not another example of the quest for immediate gratification in Caribbean societies.[10] Baptist leaders are very selective in their overspending. They scrupulously meet day-to-day operating expenses and overspend only on nonessential items. Never do they purposely place the very survival of their churches in jeopardy. Whereas they may seem frivolous with regard to telephone service, they are much more conservative on matters pertaining to physical maintenance of the church building. They do not order building materials on credit if they do not feel confident that they will be able to pay for them. As one leader put it: "You don't start a new foundation until you have enough cement."

Many church leaders do not own the land upon which their

building has been constructed, and they must pay rent for its use. Leaders are very conscientious in meeting this obligation and, for this reason, are considered good tenants. Generally, rent is nominal (especially if the landlord or members of his family are Spiritual Baptists); however, it is high when one considers these buildings are used only one or two days a week. Although rates must conform to government regulations, rental fees in Curepe range from fifty dollars a month to one hundred twenty dollars a month.

Differences in rent also reflect differing attitudes toward the Baptists. Some landlords are sympathetic to the faith, believing that it is advantageous for them to have Baptists on their property. Leaders recite special prayers and perform rites of purification to protect landlords and their families from orisha. On the other hand, some landlords fear the Baptists. They are uneasy concerning their presence and, for the most part, would just as soon evict them but for fear of the consequences. Few Trinidadians own land, and laws tend to favor renters over landlords. Several Baptist churches in Port of Spain registered civil suits to keep from being evicted and won.

Some aspects of church operations are not easily classified as expenditures or revenues. Ostensibly, mourning and baptismal ceremonies are separate from church budgets and are self-sustaining operations paid for by their participants. In practice, however, churches may lose or gain money on these rites.

Candidates for mourning and baptism make all arrangements directly with their spiritual leaders. There are two ways to pay for the service: (1) in-kind, in which case the leader provides the candidate with a list of all he/she will need for the ceremony, and the candidate purchases all items at local stores; or (2) by set-rate, in which case the leader demands a predetermined amount of money from each candidate and provides all necessary items. In both cases, any surplus should be returned to the candidate. In practice, surpluses are kept as a donation to the church or appropriated by leaders for their own use.

Baptism and mourning rites are expensive. Set-rates vary from one hundred twenty dollars to two hundred fifty dollars in Curepe and, depending on the reputation of the leader, may cost as much as a thousand dollars elsewhere on the island. Because mourning rites last a week or more, they are more expensive than baptisms. Candidates are expected to provide food for themselves and their supervisors—sometimes as many as six persons. Mourners themselves undergo periods of fasting, while leaders, mothers, and nurses eat three or four meals a day. Added expense is incurred as candles are supposed to be burned twenty-four hours a day for the duration of the ceremony. If leaders adhere strictly to this practice, several hundred candles may be burned within a week.

Many items supplied for the mourning ceremony make their way into general church operations. Mourners, for example, are requested to supply twelve-inch tapered candles like those that are usually burned during public worship. Mothers and leaders, however, sometimes substitute cheaper—about twelve cents each—locally made candles. In addition, mourners supply high-quality food (instructions to candidates paying in-kind are so specific as to include brand names), but mothers feed helpers other foods instead; thus, many communal feasts and ceremonial meals are sponsored indirectly by mourners. While some candidates may be aware of these practices, they do not openly express their objections. Since they are blindfolded and supposedly in a state of spiritual elevation, they should be unconcerned with worldly things and it would be unseemly for them to complain.

Even small surpluses from the mourning ceremony are important because churches operate on a very tight margin. Although certain periods in the fiscal year, especially those immediately following a successful pilgrimage, are characterized by relative affluence, Baptists do not hold onto their money. In the course of a year, most churches seem to spend more than they earn.

A sample 1976 church budget for the Mt. C. church in Curepe (taken from the paramount leader's diary) (see Table 6) illustrates their very small margin in economic affairs. This budget seems rather low and may not be representative of all Baptist churches in Trinidad or even in Curepe, but I believe it is accurate for the church in question. Losses, in this case a deficit of $209TT ($92US), are carried over to the next year's budget. Usually the first pil-

Table 6
A SAMPLE CHURCH BUDGET, CUREPE, 1976

Expenditures	
Rent ($60/month)	$ 720
Ritual (candles and incense)	600
Utilities (electricity, telephone)	144
Miscellaneous (maintenance, vestments, etc.)	200
Total	$ 1,664
Income	
Offerings	$ 504
Pilgrimages	913
Missions	38
Total	$ 1,455

grimage of any given year is to cover debts from the previous year.

Of the expenses listed in the budget, rent is considered the most vital, and there is little flexibility in making monthly payments. Some landlords permit churches to get several months behind but will not tolerate much more than that. Many churches are situated on potentially valuable (commercially zoned) property, and landlords cannot afford to turn down better offers for the use of the location. Churches located on prime real estate are reluctant to get behind in their rent because a great deal of status is derived from occupying such space. High rent is yet another form of conspicuous consumption.

If churches must cut their expenses, they usually do so in the areas of ritual and utilities. Paramount leaders may lessen ritual expenses by scheduling services every other week or, in extreme circumstances, cutting down on the length of services. They may also substitute cheaper ritual items in worship; however, most church leaders would prefer to hold service every other week rather than curtail the length of ceremonies or make substitutions.

Utilities are a flexible expense. Electricity and telephone service constitute luxuries because churches may function well without either. The luxury status of telephone service has already been discussed. Actually, electricity is not more vital for day-today operations. Night services, rarely held, do not require electric lights because they are traditionally held by candlelight. The only real use for electricity in Spiritual Baptist churches is to power amplifiers and sound systems.

Miscellaneous expenses, by and large, cannot be cut, but they can be transferred to a leader's personal expenses. Many leadership expenses cannot be altered (purchase of new vestments, Bibles, etc.). Churches are willing to pay the bulk of these expenses out of general operating budgets; however, if they find themselves unable to do so, they will expect their leaders to carry on the above responsibilities out of the leaders' own pockets.

Foreign Missions

For a small number of churches, a major church expenditure is the support of foreign missions. Since no Curepe churches were directly involved in missionary activity at the time of my research, I was unable to include missions in discussions of church budgets. Data on missions are taken primarily from informants in San Juan and Daberdie, whose churches maintain mission fields in Venezuela.

Baptists sponsor missions throughout the Americas, with special attention to Toronto (Canada), New York City, Aruba, and Venezuela. There are also reports of missionary work in Georgetown, Guyana, in cooperation with a local group, the Jordanites. Each site has a large Trinidadian population, but area Trinidadians are not the focus of these campaigns. Many leaders "commission" members who are visiting relatives in a given area to spend some time handing out tracts. On other occasions, leaders will purchase plane tickets for fifteen or twenty loyal members to go on mission in a given area. These missions, as may be surmised, are much more expensive.

Proselytizing techniques in foreign missions are similar to those utilized in local street missions. Missionaries often arrive in an area completely unprepared for what they may encounter. Missionaries to Venezuela, for example, rarely learn Spanish. It is thought that the particular "truth" they offer will transcend linguistic barriers and that the truth will be heard whether or not potential converts are able to understand what is being said. In the case of Venezuela, there are substantial pockets of English-speaking West Indians along the coast, but no attempts are made to take advantage of this. Sites are chosen irrespective of racial, ethnic, or linguistic considerations.

Baptists pay scant attention to the content of tracts they distribute. While leaders are mindful of artwork, format, printing quality, and layout, they evidence little regard for the message. Resourceful leaders correspond widely, requesting tracts from any American denomination at a nominal price. It appears to make minimal difference whether literature represents the theological positions of Mormons, Seventh Day Adventists, Word of God, or Presbyterians. Indeed, I have examples of all four types in my collection, given to me by a San Juan pastor.

During initial months of fieldwork, I found the diversity of tracts somewhat confusing. When questioned, leaders responded that it makes no difference what is written in the tract because people are not "convicted" by words on a page. A major reason for distributing tracts is so potential converts will have something tangible to help them remember the encounter.

While many types of tracts are available free of charge, Spiritual Baptists prefer to use fancy multicolored ones that must be paid for in cash. One provisional budget for a Venezuelan campaign allowed $200TT ($94US) for purchase of suitable literature. Such expenditures are the mark of a successful campaign. It confers prestige and demonstrates a church's wealth.

Local Baptists, upon being given a tract, will attempt to determine whether the donor paid for his literature or received it gratis. If they decide the latter, they will throw it away (sometimes in sight of the donor), while if they decide the former, the tract will be a focus of much praise and attention. Baptists delight in finding new tracts, often trading them as children in the United States trade baseball cards. A rare tract may be worth more than several hundred of a common variety.

An examination of mission budget proposals for San Juan indicates that these activities may be classified as a form of luxury spending. Many tentative budgets include items such as tracts and ritual paraphernalia already available at the site (usually at lesser cost). Moreover, when the campaign is finished, many such items are left behind. Conservation measures, such as inexpensive accommodations for participants, stem more from personal notions of sacrifice than a true desire to economize. In fact, leaders boast to one another about how much they spent on a particular campaign. My own feeling, shared by many Baptists, is that missions serve as a means of demonstrating the "success" of one's church much more than they serve as a means of attracting new converts.

Foreign missions provide another example of the complexity of economic life, and there is reason to believe that economic affairs may have been even more complex in the 1920s and 1930s when many churches functioned as self-sufficient communes. The last Baptist commune in La Roman folded in 1936, and there are few records available for this period. In the 1960s several unsuccessful attempts were made to reactivate communal groupings in the Belmont section of Port of Spain. Commitment to the concept, however, was not very strong. Informants assure me that Spiritual Baptists have always been flexible and innovative in economic affairs and that they have always risen to meet new challenges. The data I have gathered, while far from complete, provide ample evidence for this assertion.

• Conclusions

IN THIS ethnography I have provided a description of Spiritual Baptist activities in Trinidad. While the Baptists possess a unique and fascinating faith, I have not tried to sensationalize their religion. My focus throughout has been on the stuff of daily life—political squabbles, rules of succession, payment of rent—that is, things that differentiate successful leaders and less successful leaders.

Those researchers who preceded me in the field examined the religion almost exclusively within the framework of New World African retentions. In *Trinidad Village*, Melville Herskovits and Frances Herskovits presented the first and by far the most influential treatment of the religious group.[1] Their work was primarily a community study of Toco, an isolated village on the northwest coast, and only one chapter was devoted to the Baptists. Their emphasis on Africanisms led them to interpret Baptist ritual as essentially a "reinterpretation" of Shango, but the religion they described, especially mourning and baptism ceremonies, is clearly the same religion I studied.

While there is much potential in the Herskovitses' approach, I found that very little of what I observed in Trinidad could be explained in terms of Africa. The Baptists have been greatly influenced by other island religions, and many aspects of church organization can best be seen as a response to a highly advanced capitalist economy. Their acquisitiveness, for example, may be partially attributed to their booming economic situation. The religion must be seen in context and not as simply a remnant of an African past. African elements are present, but these elements are only a part of the whole.

Many Baptist leaders, in their quest for respectability, have tried to downplay African elements within the faith. Several Curepe informants, commenting on the published accounts of Herskovits and Simpson, complained that the accounts do not make their religion appear "as the other faiths" (by which they meant London Baptists, Presbyterians, Anglicans, and so on). One leader, who was extremely anxious that my book should "set things right," was very careful lest I visit churches with Shango connections and get the "wrong impression." Ironically, his own church had Shango connections, and so he did not take me there.

In this study I hope to have conveyed something of the tremendous diversity within the Baptist belief system, but in diversity I have also noted considerable unity. People who do not share the same beliefs—even people whose beliefs may appear antithetical, such as Shangoists and non-Shangoists—participate in rituals together. Moreover, I found that people of similar beliefs do not tend to belong to the same churches. Every church has within its membership a broad spectrum of belief and practice.

Baptists do not overlook theological differences. They are very much aware of such differences; for example, at every service they debate alternate interpretations of scripture. Leaders openly criticize one another, and, non-Shangoists frequently publicly denounce Shangoists. Still, Baptists participate in mourning ceremonies, baptisms, and pilgrimages together with individuals whose theological positions they claim to despise.

Tolerance for divergent beliefs is much more common in Trinidad (and elsewhere in the Caribbean) than it is in Europe and parts of North America. Perhaps this relates to the tradition of religious and cultural pluralism on the island. It may also relate to the tolerance associated with African[2] and Asian religions. Sect formation in Europe was very much interrelated with social, economic, and political movements—movements that have little meaning for Trinidadians who received Christianity secondhand through missionaries. Trinidadian Methodists, Anglicans, and Presbyterians have little stake in theological differences that separate Methodists, Anglicans, and Presbyterians in Europe. This, I believe, also leads to greater tolerance.

The Spiritual Baptists illustrate what Durkheim saw as the immense power of ritual in creating and maintaining social solidarity and religious identity[3] but also illustrate that ritual can maintain solidarity *without maintaining consensus*. In Chapter 3, I stated that all Baptist churches are united by baptism and mourning rites but pointed out that all Baptists do not share in the meanings of these rites.

With the exception of baptism and mourning rituals, leaders enjoy considerable latitude in the performance of church ritual. I have tried to show that ritual adoptions and deletions are solely the prerogatives of paramount leaders, whose decisions concerning ritual change are most frequently calculated in terms of recruitment goals. Leaders add rituals that they believe will attract new members to their services. If a leader desires to attract Pentecostals, he will add Pentecostal-style rituals—most commonly exorcisms. Such additions, Baptists claim, may add to a church's appeal and increase a leader's prestige within the faith.

Ritual additions and deletions, I found, often conform to what Bastide has called the principle of juxtaposition.[4] Other researchers noted considerable syncretism of African and Christian elements within the Baptist religion, but at the time of my fieldwork I noted considerable temporal and spatial separation of African and Christian elements. I have suggested that such juxtaposition may be understood as an attempt by leaders to maximize their power. According to Baptist belief, every ritual has its greatest power in its original content; and, by spatial and temporal separation, Baptist leaders attempt to preserve each ritual intact. It may be, as Laguerre asserts, that it is better to rely on two magics rather than one,[5] but Baptists contend that the two magics must be separated so as to retain their respective efficacies.

Differences in ritual adoption were noted between experienced and inexperienced paramount leaders. Inexperienced leaders were less likely to adopt new rituals into their services; and when they did adopt new rituals, they performed them with utmost care. Experienced leaders, on the other hand, adopted new rituals freely and were very relaxed in performing the rituals. The scrupulosity of the former may have been an attempt to make up for what they lacked in terms of credentials.

Similar tendencies were also observed in Spiritual Baptist music. There are two dominant forms of Baptist music: (1) antiphonal[6] and (2) improvisational. The antiphonal form is highly structured (the leader sings a line, the congregation repeats the line, the leader sings the next line, the congregation repeats it, and so on). The improvisational form allows for greater spontaneity and has been compared to American jazz. The leader sets a tone or beat, and other members of the congregation take off from there. Leaders who have been in power for less than five years seem to prefer the antiphonal style, but more experienced leaders are much more open to musical innovation.

Differences noted in musical form are also apparent in other aspects of church life. In churches where the antiphonal form predominates, boundaries are rigidly defined, and there are strict criteria for membership. In churches where the improvisational form predominates, boundaries are loose, and anyone can join the church.[7] Neither form is seen as the ideal. Baptist informants recognize differences but say that they "appreciates both." Members seem to experience minimal difficulty in going from one type of church to the other. This is not surprising because people of many other cultures (including my own) make similar transitions as part of daily life.

Even in the most lax of churches, it would be incorrect to classify Baptist organizations as "democratic" or "equalitarian."[8] In Chapters 4 and 5, an extremely complex organizational hierarchy was outlined. While Baptists differ as to their own positions within the hierarchy, all Baptists acknowledge that such a hierarchy exists. The firm control that paramount leaders exercise over promotion decisions, church finances, and most other aspects of church life belie whatever equalitarian sentiments or tendencies other researchers may have noted.

A leader's authority cannot be understood exclusively in terms of charismatic or traditional legitimacy (at least not as these terms were understood by Max Weber). Each leader's authority is based on a combination of factors, and these factors change over a leader's lifespan. Junior leaders, it was found, exercise limited authority on the basis of their charisma, while more senior leaders exercise greater authority on the basis of tradition. The strongest form of legitimacy, however, is that inherent in property rights. Leaders who owned their buildings outright enjoyed greater autonomy than did most other leaders.

Leaders in my sample sacrificed a great deal to attain and maintain their positions. It must be emphasized that these positions are valued in and of themselves—not because benefits accrue directly to their holders. I estimate that most Baptist leaders lose money on their religious activities. For the successful leader, attainment of high religious office has been the most important thing in his life. In the words of one informant, "When I be at work, I be thinkin' about my church. . . . when I be at the table, I be thinkin' about my church. . . . and when it be time for bed, I be thinkin' about my church. A leader have no life but his church."

Promotion in the faith does not depend upon personal revelations but on how these revelations are interpreted by church leaders. This calls into question the relationship between charisma and authority because even those who claim divine revelation must have these revelations accepted by others. Moreover, promotion decisions, like other leadership decisions, are calculated. Many factors are taken into account, including: a candidate's relative wealth, his or her prior purchase of pilgrimage tickets, special talents and skills, and the current institutional needs of the church (Is there a shortage of church nurses? Does the church need a new bellringer or surveyor?). Ecstatic experience, I concluded, is not primary consideration in these decisions.

I suggested in my introduction that men and women have very different perspectives on the faith. Men are by and large concerned with the institutional church, while women are by and large concerned with religious experience. Male-female differences were noted in other aspects of church life. Women, for example, may not speak from the pulpit, and in many church rites, such as baptism and mourning, they take a less active role. Even if a woman "owns" a church building, she needs a male to perform ritual and take care of church operations. Nevertheless, it would be incorrect to conclude that women are denigrated in the Baptist religion. Women's contributions are highly valued. I was repeatedly told that male and female roles are complementary. Just as a woman cannot run a church on her own, men cannot perform rites of baptism and mourning without the help of nurses and mothers. Men and women simply exercise authority in different terms.

Lieber, in his discussion of Trinidadian sex roles, notes that Trinidadian men of all classes approach women first and foremost as objects to be manipulated; after that, as objects of contempt.[9] I do not find this to be true for Spiritual Baptist leaders. While Baptist leaders do manipulate women, they do not deal with them contemptuously. Women are not seen as equals, but a prevailing attitude of Spiritual Baptist men toward women is one of respect. In the words of one Baptist leader, "We had to respect them 'cause womans can do thing that we [men] cannot."

One area in which men never acknowledge women's contributions is fund raising. Church economics are entirely the concern of males, and, as noted, primarily the responsibility of the paramount leader. While paramount leaders may seek advice from other high-ranking churchmen, it is they who must "build" their churches. In Chapter 5, I demonstrated that paramount leaders do not run their church finances in accordance with the principles of rational captialism and that they are expected to take risks in order to show that they have been "chosen" by God the Father. Successful leaders in my sample frequently purchased luxury items, such as speakers and amplifiers, that went well beyond their church budgets.

In order to meet the costs of regular and luxury expenditures, leaders rely on profits from a unique form of fund raising, the pilgrimage. Pilgrimages—as leaders themselves acknowledge—are not the most direct way of raising money. Most leaders in my sample stated that they would prefer to raise funds by general offerings but that this would not be possible. Two questions must be raised with respect to fund raising: (1) Why do Baptists not contribute more during general offerings? (2) Why do Baptists continue to purchase pilgrimage tickets, even though the cost of pilgrimage tickets have more than tripled since 1976?

The answers to these questions become clearer when pilgrimages are seen from a decision-making perspective. Baptists do not contribute more in weekly offerings because weekly offerings are collected anonymously and the contributors get no recognition for their gifts. Leaders claim that they do not keep track of weekly offerings because these offerings are too small to command their attention. They do, however, keep careful records of pilgrimage tickets (with some records going back ten years or more). Members calculate that they will obtain greater recognition for purchase of pilgrimage tickets than could be obtained by offerings and so have decided to give to their churches in this manner.

The preceding chapters have demonstrated that the Baptists do not fit the typology of Caribbean religions suggested by I.M. Lewis.[10] The Baptists are not, as Lewis postulated, a "peripheral cult" disguising itself as a healing cult. Members of the faith take active roles in Trinidadian society. Lewis also suggested that religions like the Baptists are a primary means of redress against thwarted ambitions and serve as a vehicle of protest against the established order. My data indicate that the Baptists now possess other, more effective means of airing their grievances and that the church is central—not peripheral—to island life.[11]

The Spiritual Baptist church is a viable religious tradition on the island and will remain viable for many years. Not all researchers share my opinion. Simpson, contending that as Trinidadians become more affluent they will cease to support the faith, predicts a serious decline in membership.[12] The predicted decline has not materialized. My data suggest that the church in Trinidad is growing slightly and is attracting more affluent members of the society, including East Indians and creoles.

In the first half of this century many Baptists appear to have associated Christianity and respectability, but this changed with the advent of Black Power in the 1960s. Many younger Baptist leaders now associate respectability with African-derived religions, such as Shango. As these younger men begin to occupy positions of church authority, Shango may come to have a dominant position in a larger number of churches on the island, and so-called Christian elements of the religion will be less emphasized.

Another change is that there may be a shift in the center of Spiritual Baptist operations. Baptists in Trinidad are not community based. Most members attend churches some distance from their places of residence. Mobility, however, is not confined to the church membership. Many of the most able Spiritual Baptist leaders are also mobile, leaving Trinidad to occupy paid positions in Spiritual Baptist churches in the United States and Canada. A similar movement occurred in the early years of this century when Baptist leaders migrated from St. Vincent to Trinidad. A primary inducement was money. Wages were higher in Trinidad, and churches in Trinidad were thought to provide more opportunities for those desiring leadership positions. Today, it is churches in North America that are thought to provide more opportunities for advancement.

What are the implications of this for the Trinidad Church? There is—and will continue to be—something of a leadership drain as many of the most ambitious and experienced Spiritual Baptist leaders leave Trinidad; however, the Baptists will be able to weather this better than other religious groups because there are so many individuals within the Baptist organization who desire to become leaders; all (or most) male members want to become paramount leaders themselves.

Acculturation is a two-way street, and in the coming years Spiritual Baptist churches in the United States and Canada will have a tremendous influence on Baptist churches in Trinidad. As overseas pastors return to visit their old congregations, they will bring with them new ideas and ritual innovations. One area in which this is already occurring is in Spiritual Baptist music.

In 1976, I interviewed a Baptist leader in St. Vincent who complained of the excesses and commercialism of Spiritual Baptist churches in Trinidad. He asserted that Trinidad churches had "traveled in the wrong direction" and was resentful that St. Vincent—where, he contended, the faith had originated—was no longer the center of Baptist operations. If the church catches on among West Indians in North America, it will not be too many years before Trinidadian Baptist leaders begin making similar statements about North American Baptist churches.

I predict that the Spiritual Baptists will experience some successes in their North American campaigns, not with their missionary endeavors per se but among Caribbean emigrants. Baptist leadership is aggressive and ambitious; and because the faith has already adapted to the advanced industrial economy of Trinidad, it should have minimal difficulty in adapting to the advanced industrial economies of the United States and Canada.

• *Appendix: Shango Rites*

MY INITIAL impression of Shango was that it is so different from the Baptists that close association between the two religions would be unlikely. While Baptists stress the Christian Bible and possession by the Holy Ghost, Shango is derived from an African tradition and emphasizes possession by a number of spirit beings. Nevertheless, I later confirmed Simpson's assertion that these religions are closely related.[1]

The belief system of Shango, like that of the Baptists, has incorporated gods from a number of diverse religious traditions. A major ceremony or feast is given by each Shango leader at least once a year. During this ceremony the gods are called by singing and drumming. While many people attend Shango ceremonies as spectators, usually only a few individuals (six to ten) actually become possessed by the gods. This contrasts with the Baptists, who encourage a greater number of participants to become possessed by the Holy Ghost.

A Shango cult center consists of a shrine area where five or ten "stools" for the most important powers or spirits are located, a "chapelle" or small cult house, and a "palais" where public ceremonies are held. "Stools" are concrete mounds raised six to twelve inches, on which are placed candles, a pot of water, a flag, and one or more of the god's implements (to be discussed). A "chapelle" is the storage area where ritual items (candles, cutlasses, daggers, hammers, olive oil, flower vases, etc.) are kept, and a "palais" is an open-air structure with a galvanized roof and concrete floor. Benches on all four sides of the palais provide limited seating for spectators. All but the most important guests stand for much of the duration of the ceremony. Most

Shango centers also have a large open kitchen where food is prepared.

All Shango ceremonies are sponsored by individuals who must make preparations and bear all expenses themselves. An elaborate four-day service may cost as much as four thousand dollars. Three services in Tunapuna cost twenty-five hundred, twenty-nine hundred, and twenty-seven hundred dollars, respectively. Attendance at these Tunapuna services ranged from two or three hundred persons each night. This resulted in considerable expense for sponsors of the ceremonies, who were obliged to provide food for all participants and spectators at regular intervals.

No one is barred from attending Shango ceremonies. There are three rules, however, that must be observed: (1) one must not be disruptive, (2) one must not smoke, and (3) one must not cross one's arms or legs. These same rules have been noted for other Afro-American religions.[2] Everyone who obeys these rules must be fed, and some sponsors complain that many persons attend Shango solely "for the refreshments."

Shango cult centers are dominated by their leader-sponsors, and all who attend services are expected to follow his direction. Mischel, Clement, and Simpson claim that the sponsor-leader for a given community is known as that community's *amombo* or *amumba* ("one who carries the feast"),[3] although leaders in the Curepe area prefer the title "King" usually followed by their surnames.

Major rites for each chapelle are scheduled to take place between June and November. The summer months are particularly popular times for such services, since Shango feasts can be made to correspond with one's annual vacation from work. Some leaders, especially in the South, now hold services in December and April. Leaders state that this is because it is no longer imperative that a particular feast correspond with a particular saint's feast day. In services I attended, there was almost no mention of saints. The most important consideration in scheduling a Shango service, according to some informants, was that a time be found that does not conflict with another leader's ceremony.

An entire Shango feast takes from two to four days, depending on the resources of the sponsor. In Tunapuna and San Juan, services were sponsored for the full four days. They began on Tuesday evening (about five o'clock) and concluded on Saturday night. Ideally, services should be concluded before midnight on Saturdays so as not to run over into the sabbath; however, Saturday is usually the night with the largest attendance, and few services disband before the early morning. People who attend Shango past midnight are not supposed to attend Spiritual Baptist worship on the next day.

Shango services begin with a prayer meeting.[4] Prayer meetings are held away from the palais (usually in another community). The Catholic church does not permit known Shango leaders to hold prayer meetings in their churches, and therefore many leaders who would prefer to hold prayers in a Catholic church sponsor these meetings in Spiritual Baptist churches. For leaders who are also active in the Spiritual Baptist faith, a reciprocal arrangement is worked out with a neighboring church (never one's own). For leaders who are not active in the Spiritual Baptist religion, payment must be made for use of Spiritual Baptist facilities. Some Baptist leaders will not rent space to known Shango sponsors. Other Baptists take a laissez-faire attitude, claiming, "We don' care what they does longs they's gots moneys dats good." As mentioned previously, most Shango leaders have Spiritual Baptist affiliations, while many Spiritual Baptists do not have Shango affiliations.

Sometimes Shango leaders conduct prayer meetings themselves. Most of the time, however, they ask the Baptist leader associated with that church to perform them. When a leader performs his own prayer meetings, he is in what one Baptist leader described as a "most discomfortable" position— he is a celebrant in two religious traditions at the same time. This is thought to be dangerous because at a later date the African powers might question his "sincerity."

In Tunapuna, opening prayers are held on a different day than the Shango ceremony itself. At the very least there should be five or six hours between opening prayers and the actual ceremony. It should also be noted that few individuals attend opening prayers. One leader in Belmont no longer sponsors the prayers at all. He claims that the last Spiritual Baptist service he attended (no matter how long ago) serves as his opening prayers.

For many, prayers are no longer an important part of Shango. When asked why leaders continue to sponsor them, the most common response was that it had always been done that way. "African gods don' needs prayer," I was told.

At the palais, Ogun, the Yoruban god of iron, is summoned first. The drummers play his rhythm (which seems to vary from center to center) and one of his songs is sung. After a long period of drumming (several hours), Ogun finally arrives to possess his devotee. Ideally, other powers should not arrive prior to Ogun. In practice, several devotees are usually in trance before Ogun appears; however, they should remain on the sidelines in deference to Ogun. Also, for every god there are several devotees who claim to manifest that god. The leader-sponsor of the ceremony must decide when Ogun (as opposed to a pretender) has actually arrived.

According to Mischel, the gods are expected to manifest themselves in a set order: Ogun, Omela, Gabriel, Shankpara, Osain, Shango, and Aireelay.[5] To my knowledge, this order is not followed in Tunapuna or San Juan. Most leaders admitted that this was the case and also acknowledged that there was little that they could do about it. Specific songs, for example, are supposed to induce possession by specific powers, but the powers can come and go as they please. A song for Oshun may bring another god entirely.

New powers are being adopted into the faith each year. In order to be adopted, a power must be recognized by the leader of a given center, and regional variations are important. Mahabil, who has many devotees in the South and in Port of Spain, is not recognized in Tunapuna or San Juan. In Tunapuna, when a power manifests claiming to be Mahabil, he is dismissed as an "orisha."

Shango ceremonies are extremely repetitious. Once the "real" Ogun has come, drumming, singing, spirit possession, and dancing occur all night, with occasional breaks for food. The climax of service comes at dawn, when animal sacrifice takes place (usually a chicken or a goat). Shango sponsors are very sensitive concerning animal sacrifice. They are quick to point out that the animal is not wasted but served as food the following night. In Tunapuna, animal sacrifice is not performed publicly.

It occurs behind closed doors and away from the palais. In other parts of the island no attempt is made to hide this activity.

The musical instruments used in Shango ritual consist of a set of three drums and from three to a dozen pairs of chac-chacs.[6] The drums are made of cedar, and the largest is played with one stick, while the smaller drums are played with two sticks. The drums are covered with goat skin held in place by twine rather than by pegs. Simpson notes that unlike the drums used in Haitian vodun or in the Rada cult, these instruments are double- rather than single-headed.[7] Handbells (as found in Baptist worship) are never present at Shango ceremonies.

At a Shango service, participants "dance" by rocking back and forth in time to the drumming, bending and straightening, clapping, and circling the palais (similar to a Conga line). When an individual is possessed by a particular power, he waves the implement associated with that power. For Ogun, for example, the associated implement is a sword, while for Shankpara it is a broom. The possessed also speak, serving as a "mouthpiece" for their particular power. Such speech may be in an unknown language (similar to the glossolalia of Baptist services), "Yoruba" (a mixture of African, French Creole, and English words), or plain English. Many powers will answer questions from (individual) spectators.

Leaders are expected to control all aspects of ritual and to keep watch over all participants. Rarely does a leader-sponsor ever become possessed at his own ceremony. A major function of leaders is to keep powers from "punishing" devotees by causing them to be thrown to the ground. They are also given responsibility to make certain that spectators are not injured by swords, cutlasses, daggers, flaming torches, etc. during the rites. It a spectator is injured, he or she may bring a suit against the sponsor of the ceremony.

● Notes

Preface

1. Michael Garfield Smith, *Corporations and Society: The Social Anthropology of Collective Action* (Chicago: Aldine, 1975).
2. Melville J. Herskovits and Frances S. Herskovits, *Trinidad Village* (New York: Alfred A. Knopf, 1947); George Eaton Simpson, "Baptismal, 'Mourning' and 'Building' Ceremonies of the Shouters in Trinidad," *Journal of American Folklore* 79 (1966):537-550; George Eaton Simpson, *Black Religions in the New World* (New York: Columbia University Press, 1978).
3. Fredrik Barth, *Political Leadership Among the Swat Pathans* (London: Athlone Press, 1959). For a discussion of the usefulness of this approach, see Robert L. Bee, *Patterns and Processes: An Introduction to Anthropological Strategies for the Study of Sociocultural Change* (New York: Free Press, 1974), 196-222.

Introduction

1. Melville J. Herskovits and Frances S. Herskovits, *Trinidad Village* (New York: Alfred A. Knopf, 1947).
2. George Eaton Simpson, "Baptismal, 'Mourning' and 'Building' Ceremonies of the Shouters in Trinidad," *Journal of American Folklore* 79 (1966):537-550.
3. Archbishop Griffith, in an interview in the June 14, 1973, *Sunday Guardian*, stated that there were seventy-two churches and 50,000 members in his Spiritual Baptist denomination alone. There are three other Spiritual Baptist denominations in Trinidad.
    Alfrieta Parks accepts Archbishop Griffith's estimate; however, I found it very difficult to estimate the number of Baptists because individual Baptists attend many different churches. Everywhere I went, I saw

many of the same people. For this reason, I have concluded that membership is much smaller than 50,000. Cf. Alfrieta V. Parks, "The Conceptualization of Kinship Among the Spiritual Baptists of Trinidad," Ph.D. dissertation, Princeton University, 1981, 27. This discussion will be resumed in Chapter 4.

4. See Appendix for a discussion of Shango.

5. Melville J. Herskovits, *The Myth of the Negro Past* (New York: Harper and Brothers, 1941), 223.

6. Erika Bourguignon, ed., *Religion, Altered States of Consciousness, and Social Change* (Columbus: Ohio State University Press, 1973). Other recent contributions to the literature on trance and possession states among the Spiritual Baptists include: Jeannette H. Henney, "Spirit-Possession Belief and Trance Behavior in Two Fundamentalist Groups in St. Vincent," in *Trance, Healing and Hallucination: Three Field Studies in Religious Experience*, ed. Felicitas D. Goodman, Jeannette H. Henney, and Esther Pressel (New York: John Wiley and Sons, 1974), 6-111; William Sargant, *The Mind Possessed: A Physiology of Possession, Mysticism and Faith Healing* (Philadelphia: Lippincott, 1974); Colleen Ward and Michael Beaubrun, "Trance Induction and Hallucination in Spiritual Baptist Mourning," *Journal of Psychological Anthropology* 2 (1979):479-488.

7. George Eaton Simpson, *Cult Music of Trinidad* (New York: Folkways Records and Service Corporation, 1961), FE 4478, 4.

8. Jeannette H. Henney, "Spirit-Possession Belief and Trance Behavior," 29.

9. Philip H. Ennis, "Ecstasy in Everyday Life," *Journal for the Scientific Study of Religion* 6 (1967):40-48.

10. Michael Lieber, *Street Scenes: Afro-American Culture in Urban Trinidad* (Cambridge, Mass.: Schenkman Publishing Company, 1981).

11. Roger Bastide, *The African Religions of Brazil: Toward a Sociology of the Interpenetration of Civilizations* (Baltimore: Johns Hopkins University Press, 1978), 278; Herskovits, *The Myth of the Negro Past*.

12. Frances Osterman Mischel, "A Shango Religious Group and the Problem of Prestige in Trinidadian Society," Ph.D. dissertation, Ohio State University, 1958; George Eaton Simpson, *Religious Cults of the Caribbean* (Rio Piedras, P.R.: Institute of Caribbean Studies, 1970); Dorothy Caye Clement, "Shango: A Modernizing Cult in Trinidadian Society," M.A. thesis, University of North Carolina at Chapel Hill, 1969, 35.

13. Franz Cumont, *Oriental Religions in Roman Paganism* (New York: Dover Press, 1956).

14. Ioan M. Lewis, *Ecstatic Religion: An Anthropological Study of Spirit Possession and Shamanism* (Middlesex, Eng.: Penguin Books, 1971).

15. Roger Bastide, *African Civilizations in the New World* (New York: Harper and Row, 1971).
16. Richard Price, ed., *Maroon Societies: Rebel Slave Communities in the Americas* (Baltimore: Johns Hopkins University Press, 1979), 29-30.

1. The Setting

1. Linda A. Newson, *Aboriginal and Spanish Colonial Trinidad: A Study in Culture Contact* (New York: Academic Press, 1976); Alfredo E. Figueredo and Stephen D. Glazier, "A Revised Aboriginal Ethnohistory of Trinidad," *Proceedings of the Seventh International Congress for the Study of Pre-Columbian Cultures in the Lesser Antilles* (Montreal: Centre de Recherches Caraibes, 1978), 259-262.
2. St. Clair Drake, "The African Diaspora in Pan-African Perspective," *Black Scholar* 7 (1975):2-13.
3. Melville J. Herskovits and Frances S. Herskovits, *Trinidad Village* (New York: Alfred A. Knopf, 1947), 305.
4. Michael Anthony, *Profile Trinidad: A Historical Survey from Discovery to 1900* (London: Macmillan-Caribbean, 1975), 89; John O. Stewart, "Mission and Leadership Among the 'Meriken' Baptists of Trinidad," *Contributions to the Latin American Anthropology Group*, ed. Norman Whitten (Washington, D.C.: Latin American Anthropology Group, 1976), 17-25.
5. *West Indies and Caribbean Yearbook, 1977*, 343.
6. Bridget Brereton, *A History of Modern Trinidad, 1783-1962* (London: Heinemann, 1981); Selwyn C. Ryan, *Race and Nationalism in Trinidad and Tobago: A Study of Decolonization in a Multiracial Society* (Toronto: University of Toronto Press, 1972).
7. Yogendra Kuman Malik, *East Indians in Trinidad: A Study in Minority Politics* (New York: Oxford University Press, 1971).
8. Frances Osterman Mischel, "A Shango Religious Group and the Problem of Prestige in Trinidadian Society," Ph.D. dissertation, Ohio State University, 1958; Ioan M. Lewis, *Ecstatic Religion: An Anthropological Study of Spirit Possession and Shamanism* (Middlesex, Eng.: Penguin Books, 1971).
9. Bridget Brereton, *Race Relations in Colonial Trinidad, 1870-1900* (New York: Cambridge University Press, 1979); Eric Williams, *The Negro in the Caribbean* (Manchester, Eng.: Manchester University Press, 1946). See Farley S. Brathwaite, "Race and Class Differentials in Career (Value) Orientation," *Plural Societies* 7 (1976):17-31. Brathwaite concludes that, in respect to career orientation, class differences are more widespread than racial differences.
10. Ivan Oxxal, *Race and Revolutionary Consciousness: A Documentary*

Interpretation of the 1970 Black Power Revolt in Trinidad (Cambridge, Mass.: Schenkman Publishing Company, 1971).

11. Barry Chevannes, "Revivalism: A Disappearing Religion," *Caribbean Quarterly* 24 (1978):1-17; George Eaton Simpson, *Black Religions in the New World* (New York: Columbia University Press, 1978), 305.

12. Baptist leaders often claim to have baptized prominent (and not so prominent) people. I was surprised in 1979 to discover that Leader C. claimed to have baptized me in 1978. He did not.

13. Daniel J. Crowley, "Plural and Differential Acculturation in Trinidad," *American Anthropologist* 59 (1957):823.

14. Stephen D. Glazier, "Pentecostal Exorcism and Modernization in Trinidad," in *Perspectives on Pentecostalism: Case Studies from the Caribbean and Latin America* (Washington, D.C.: University Press of America, 1980), 67-80.

2. The Belief System

1. Pertti J. Pelto and Gretel Pelto, "Intra-cultural Diversity: Some Theoretical Issues," *American Ethnologist* 2 (1975):1-18.

2. Anthony F. C. Wallace, *Culture and Personality* (New York: Random House, 1961), 35-38.

3. Stuart Philpott, *West Indian Migration: The Montserrat Case* (London: Athlone, 1973).

4. Melville J. Herskovits, "African Gods and Catholic Saints in New World Negro Belief," *American Anthropologist* 39 (1937):635-643; George Eaton Simpson, *Religious Cults in the Caribbean: Trinidad, Jamaica and Haiti* (Rio Piedras, P.R.: Institute of Caribbean Studies, 1970).

5. Members of both the Rada and Shango faiths in Trinidad associate African deities and Catholic saints. Patterns of association differ markedly. Some believers identify African gods with Catholic saints but recognize that these are not the same. Other believers contend that African gods and Catholic saints are manifestations of the same gods. Many of my most thoughtful Shango informants were themselves puzzled by this. Several suggested that I should talk with Papa N. (an East Indian and former Hindu pandit) if I were "really interested" in the topic.

It is unclear exactly when African gods acquired association with Catholic saints in Trinidad. Andrew T. Carr, in personal communication, asked members of the Rada faith when their gods received their Christian names. The response was that they had "always" had them. My own inquiries to Shango leaders elicited similar responses.

6. Arthur Niehoff and Juanita Niehoff, *East Indians in the West Indies*

(Milwaukee: Milwaukee Public Museum Publications in Anthropology, 1960).

7. Other religious groups do fear lagahus; cf. Michael Garfield Smith, *Dark Puritan* (Kingston, Jamaica: Department of Extra-Mural Studies, University of the West Indies, 1962), 91.

8. Unlike the creator god in African mythology, God the Father has not, according to Baptist belief, removed himself from intimate daily contact with human beings. On the other hand, God the Father does not enter into the human body in possession of the human as do other spirits and the Holy Ghost. Baptist relations with God the Father do not seem to fit Osadolar Imasogie's description of the West African sacred cosmos as "bureaucratic monotheism." See Osadolar Imasogie, "African Traditional Religion and Christian Faith," *Review and Expositor* 70 (1973):289. The term "bureaucratic monotheism" is misleading because it does not impart the significant difference between God the Father and other spirits. See Mechal Sobel, *Trabelin' On: The Slave Journey to an Afro-Baptist Faith* (Westport, Conn.: Greenwood Press, 1979), 16.

9. In many Spiritual Baptist churches, communion is not given at all. Communion rites are most common in urban churches and churches that are members of denominational organizations. In Moruga, communion is ideally offered on the first Sunday of each month but in actuality it is offered only once or twice each year. The explanation given is that communion is sometimes cancelled because there is not enough money for bread and wine. See Alfrieta V. Parks, "The Conceptualization of Kinship Among the Spiritual Baptists of Trinidad," Ph.D. dissertation, Princeton University, 1981, 67. I find the above explanation unlikely because Baptists spend so much on other aspects of church ritual; see Chapter 5.

10. Dreams have long been regarded as a form of communication with the supernatural. This belief has been reported throughout the West Indies. In *"Glorious Liberty"*: *The Story of a Hundred Years' Work of the Jamaica Baptist Mission* (London: The Baptist Missionary Society, 1914), Leonard Tucker noted that in Jamaica "a class of religious teachers among the slaves sent people into the bush to have dreams before being baptized" (p. 55).

11. Charles Gullick, "Shakers and Ecstasy," *New Fire* 9 (1971):10.

12. I never once heard the mention of Hell or a similar place in a Spiritual Baptist sermon. Alfrieta Parks claims that Hell was not mentioned during her entire stay among the Baptists. See Parks, "The Conceptualization of Kinship Among the Spiritual Baptists of Trinidad," 18.

13. Melville J. Herskovits and Frances S. Herskovits, *Trinidad Village* (New York: Alfred A. Knopf, 1947).

14. Jeannette H. Henney, "Spirit-Possession Belief and Trance Behavior in Two Fundamentalist Groups in St. Vincent," in *Trance, Healing and Hallucination: Three Field Studies in Religious Experience*, ed. Felicitas D. Goodman, Jeannette H. Henney, and Esther Pressel (New York: John Wiley and Sons, 1974), 6-111.

15. Stephen D. Glazier, "Heterodoxy and Heteropraxy in the Spiritual Baptist Faith," *Journal of the Interdenominational Theological Center* 8 (1980):89-101.

16. Donald Wood, *Trinidad in Transition: The Years After Slavery* (New York: Oxford University Press, 1968), 240-241.

17. Andrew T. Carr, "A Rada Community in Trinidad," *Caribbean Quarterly* 3 (1953):40.

18. Smith, *Dark Puritan*, 88-89.

19. Gullick, "Shakers and Ecstasy," 10.

20. Henney, "Spirit-Possession Belief and Trance Behavior," 23.

21. Marjorie Bowen, *Wrestling Jacob* (London: William Heinemann, 1937), 255.

22. Henney, "Spirit-Possession Belief and Trance Behavior," 18.

23. Edward Bean Underhill, *The West Indies: Their Social and Religious Condition* (London: Jackson, Wolford and Hodder, 1862).

24. John O. Stewart, "Mission and Leadership Among the 'Meriken' Baptists of Trinidad," in *Contributions to the Latin American Anthropology Group*, ed. Norman Whitten (Washington, D.C.: Latin American Anthropology Group, 1976), 17-25.

Bridget Brereton in *Race Relations in Colonial Trinidad, 1870-1900* (New York: Cambridge University Press, 1979) contends that many of the "Americans" were converted to Islam by three Mandingo former-slave priests but that they later became Baptists when a United States Baptist mission started to work in the area. She believes that connections between these "Baptists" and the Spiritual Baptists are tenuous.

25. Stewart, "Mission and Leadership Among the 'Meriken' Baptists of Trinidad," 22.

26. Ibid., 24.

27. Cf. Wood, *Trinidad in Transition*.

28. Stewart, "Mission and Leadership Among the 'Meriken' Baptists of Trinidad," 21.

3. Ritual

1. Stephen D. Glazier, "Pentecostal Exorcism and Modernization in Trinidad," in *Perspectives on Pentecostalism: Case Studies from the Caribbean*

and Latin America (Washington, D.C.: University Press of America, 1980), 67-80.

2. Melville J. Herskovits, *The Myth of the Negro Past* (New York: Harper and Brothers, 1941), 223.

3. Examples of all three forms may be found in my record album, *Spiritual Baptist Music of Trinidad* (New York: Folkways Record and Service Corporation, 1980), FE 4234. Shouting or "trumpeting in the Spirit" is not a prerequisite to church advancement; in fact, in many cases, an inverse relationship between shouting and advancement exists.

4. Cf. Bennetta Jules-Rosette, "Songs and Spirit: The Use of Songs in the Management of Ritual Contexts," *Africa* 45 (1975):150-166.

5. At the Moruga church, a sketch of key acts in songs in the mourning ceremony would look as follows:

Act	Song
1. Placing the mourner on the mercy seat.	1. "I Must Believe, I Can Believe, I'm Sitting on the Mercy Seat"
2. Opening of service.	2. "Peace Be on This House"
3. Before washing of feet.	3. "Wash Me and Cleanse Me Now My Lord"
4. During washing of feet.	4. "Wash Me, But Not My Feet Alone"
5. Comfort and farewell from the congregation.	5. "I Am on My Way to the Lord"
6. Accompanying to the mourning chamber.	6. "Carry Me Away to the Burial Ground When I Die"
7. Before blinding of eyes.	7. "Take My Life and Let It Be"
8. Putting the mourner to ground.	8. "I Want to Fly to Glory"
9. Rising night.	9. "Run, Mother Mary, Run My Lord Gone to Galilee Mother Mary, Don't You Touch Me I'm Not Ascended Yet."
10. Reenacted death.	10. "Down in the Valley"
11. Prayer after death.	11. "Somebody Touched My Soul"
12. Turning in all directions.	12. 'I'm a Poor Mourning Pilgrim"

144   Notes

13. Leaving the mourner.

14. Welcome back.

13. "Elijah Went Up . . . and No Man to Hinder Me"

14. "Happy Land of Jesus"

Not all churches perform all these acts or sing all of these hymns. Alfrieta V. Parks, "The Conceptualization of Kinship Among the Spiritual Baptists of Trinidad," Ph.D. dissertation, Princeton University, 1981, 79-80.

6. As noted above, most women direct their religious attention to the center pole, while men focus their attention to the front of the church. Men usually speak from behind a pulpit alongside or directly facing the altar. In some churches all males sit to the right of the altar, and all females sit to the left, while in urban areas, mixed seating is common.

7. In Moruga, there is a variant of this ritual using a lighted candle instead of a vase. Parks, "The Conceptualization of Kinship Among the Spiritual Baptists of Trinidad," 53.

8. William Sargant, *The Mind Possessed: A Physiology of Possession, Mysticism and Faith Healing* (Philadelphia: Lippincott, 1974); Colleen Ward and Michael Beaubrun, "Trance Induction and Hallucination in Spiritual Baptist Mourning," *Journal of Psychological Anthropology* 2 (1979): 479-488; Jeannette H. Henney, "Spirit-Possession Belief and Trance Behavior in Two Fundamentalist Groups in St. Vincent," in *Trance, Healing and Hallucination: Three Field Studies in Religious Experience*, ed. Felicitas D. Goodman, Jeannette H. Henney, and Esther Pressel (New York: John Wiley and Sons, 1974), 6-111.

9. As mentioned previously, there is no concept of unity in the Godhead.

10. Baptists claim that their mourning ceremony is a reenactment of events recorded in the Book of Daniel, specifically, the following passage from chapter 10: "I, Daniel, mourned for three full weeks; I ate no savory food, I took no meat or wine, and did not anoint myself with oil until three full weeks were completed."

Correspondence is incomplete. A major difference between Daniel's experience and Baptist rites is one of duration. In Trinidad churches' rites may last from three to seven days instead of the three full weeks described in Daniel. One Curepe leader claims that when he joined the faith in 1934, ceremonies did last for three weeks; however, Melville J. Herskovits and Frances S. Herskovits report—in *Trinidad Village* (New York: Alfred A. Knopf, 1947), 204—that the time required varied with the individual: "They [mourners] do what they're told by the Spirit, but sometimes the Spirit says they must stay longer than they plan, fourteen days and not seven, or even twenty-one." No leader in Curepe is currently willing to conduct mourning ceremonies for over seven days. One reason, leaders contend, is that it is not economically feasible. If a candidate wishes to mourn for three weeks, he or she may participate in three consecutive ceremonies at different churches; however, no leader seemed to feel that a three-week rite is either necessary or desirable.

Other differences between Daniel, chapter 10, and Baptist practice are that Baptists may anoint themselves during the ceremony and that many Baptists do not fast during the rite. A mourner's diet is simple but may include some meat (usually chicken); and, while those who participate in the rite should not drink hard liquor, those who supervise candidates sometimes do consume alcoholic beverages.

Herskovits in *The Myth of the Negro Past* (New York: Harper and Brothers, 1941) focused on baptism and mourning ceremonies as African-style initiation rites. While these rites do pertain to initiation into the faith, they are not prerequisites to participation in other forms of Baptist worship. In the African context, however, initiation is conceived as mandatory; see Benjamin C. Ray, *African Religions: Symbol, Ritual and Community* (Englewood Cliffs, N.J.: Prentice-Hall, 1976). In the Baptist context, there is much more flexibility.

Albert J. Raboteau in *Slave Religions: The Invisible Institution in the Antebellum South* (New York: Oxford University Press, 1978), 29, notes that "several features of this [the Spiritual Baptist] mourning ceremony resemble the rites of cult initiation in West Africa. Death-resurrection motifs, fasting and lying quiet, reception of a new role and a new name, color symbolism, and prohibition of salt in food offerings to the gods are all similar features of initiation in West African and Brazilian cults." He cites Samuel Miller Lawton, "Religious Life of South Carolina Coastal and Sea Island Negroes," Ph.D. dissertation, George Peabody College for Teachers, 1939: "Slaves customarily spoke of the period of seeking conversion as 'mourning' and thought that it was a time when the sinner should go apart, alone, to a quiet place to struggle with his sins. . . . Similarity may be noted in Samuel Lawton's description of a practice followed in the Sea Islands which resembled the use of cloth bands in the 'mourning ground' ceremony of Spiritual Baptists in Trinidad: 'Seekers may sometimes be identified by a white cloth or string tied around the head. This is a signal that they are seeking and all are to 'leave 'em alon'.' "

11. Ward and Beaubrun, "Trance Induction and Hallucination in Spiritual Baptist Mourning," 485.

12. Anxiety and frustration are always engendered in the revelation

of inner experience, and the mourning rite is no exception. Mourners frequently complain that they do not like to tell their visions to paramount leaders because "words is not enough." Mourners seem to feel— as psychoanalysts such as Lacan have long recognized——that articulation is not the dream but the dream *manqué*. See Vincent Crapanzano, "Introduction," in *Case Studies in Spirit Possession*, ed. Vincent Crapanzano and Vivian Garrison (New York: John Wiley, 1977).

13. Spiritual Baptist visions recorded in the 1970s have very little in common with conversion experiences and visions among black Baptist groups in the United States. Mechal Sobel in *Trabelin' On: The Slave Journey to an Afro-Baptist Faith* (Westport, Conn.: Greenwood Press, 1979), 108-109, reports that there is an "ideal type" of vision with a single structure that can be reduced to eight basic elements: (1) The seeker is called by name. (2) The individual then recounts his death, saying unambiguously, "I died." (3) Two selves are seen, a "little me inside the big me." (4) The "little me" is brought to the brink of Hell and is almost lost, but (5) the call of "Mercy, Mercy, Mercy, Lord" has an immediate effect, and (6) a little white man leads the little me eastward, sometimes through terrors, from Hell to Heaven. (7) In Heaven sheep are grazing, and God, in blazing white robes, calls the individual again; promises to be in him and with him; and (8) sends him back to life, against his will, to proclaim the good news.

Some of these elements are also present in Spiritual Baptist tracts, for example, white robes, grazing sheep, and the commandment to proclaim the good news. Other elements are missing, including: direct reference to the mourner's death, the notion of the "little me inside the big me" and a description of the terrors of Hell. Also, God the Father does not speak in Spiritual Baptist mourners' visions, whereas God the Father *does* speak directly to the mourner in the Afro-Baptist tradition. In my view, differences between Spiritual Baptist and American Afro-Baptist visions are greater than their similarities. See A. P. Watson and Clifton H. Johnson, eds., *God Struck Me Dead: Religious Conversion Experiences and Autobiographies of Negro Ex-Slaves* (Philadelphia: Pilgrim Press, 1969).

14. Mourning is believed to be helpful in that regard. See George Eaton Simpson, *Religious Cults of the Caribbean: Trinidad, Jamaica and Haiti* (Rio Piedras, P.R.: Institute for Caribbean Studies, 1970), 71.

15. Andrew T. Carr, "A Rada Community in Trinidad," *Caribbean Quarterly* 3 (1953):35-54.

16. Herskovits, *Myth of the Negro Past*, 241.

17. Simpson, *Religious Cults of the Caribbean*; Wesley Wong, "Some Folk Medicinal Plants from Trinidad," *Economic Botany* 30 (1976):103-

142. Wong claims to have talked with seventy informants and to have found 186 plants in use in a single village.

18. See Horacio Fabrega and Peter K. Manning, "An Integrated Theory of Disease: Ladino-Mestizo Views of Disease in the Chiapas Highlands," *Psychosomatic Medicine* 35 (1973):223-239; George Foster, "Relationships between Spanish and Spanish-American Folk Medicine," *Journal of American Folklore* 66 (1953):201-217; Michael H. Logan, "Digestive Disorders and Plant Medicines in Highland Guatemala," in *Health and the Human Condition*, ed. Michael H. Logan and E. E. Hunt, Jr. (North Scituate, Mass.: Duxbury Press, 1978).

19. See Wong, "Some Folk Medicinal Plants from Trinidad," 104.

20. Linda A. Newson, *Aboriginal and Spanish Colonial Trinidad: A Study in Culture Contact* (New York: Academic Press, 1976).

21. Roger Bastide, *The African Religions of Brazil: Toward a Sociology of the Interpenetration of Civilizations* (Baltimore: Johns Hopkins University Press, 1978), 163.

22. Leslie G. Desmangles, "African Interpretations of the Christian Cross in Vodun," *Sociological Analysis* 38 (1977):13-24; Michel Laguerre, "An Ecological Approach to Voodoo," *Freeing the Spirit* 3 (1974):4-12.

23. Michael Horowitz and Morton Klass, "The Martiniquian East Indian Cult of Maldevidian," *Social and Economic Studies* 10 (1961):93-100.

24. Reviewing the literature on the relationship of religious organizations to their environments, James Beckford, in "Religious Organization," *Current Sociology* 21 (1973):1-170, has drawn a number of generalizations, two of which apply to the Baptist case: (1) the influence of environmental factors is felt more strongly by those religious orga nizations that have either a poorly articulated or an indistinct collective outlook, and (2) the precise effects of environmental influence are mediated for religious organizations by their leaders.

In the Baptist case, collective outlook is indistinct (as evidenced by the myriad of competing belief systems), and, as Beckford would have predicted, environmental factors (where a church is located on the island) play an important part in ritual adoption. Also, as Beckford would predict, Baptist leaders play a major role in mediating ritual change.

25. Bastide, *The African Religions of Brazil*, 279; Laguerre, "An Ecological Approach to Voodoo," 5.

26. Simpson, *Religious Cults of the Caribbean*, 146.

27. Ibid., 45.

28. Bronislaw Malinowski, *Coral Gardens and Their Magic*, 2 vols. (London: George Allen and Unwin, 1935).

29. Seth Leacock and Ruth Leacock, *Spirits of the Deep: A Study of an Afro-Brazilian Cult* (Garden City: Doubleday, 1972), 246.

4. Leadership Roles and Church Organization

1. George Eaton Simpson, *Black Religions in the New World* (New York: Columbia University Press, 1978); Jeannette H. Henney, "The Shakers of St. Vincent: A Stable Religion," in *Religion, Altered States of Consciousness, and Social Change*, ed. Erika Bourguignon (Columbus: Ohio State University Press, 1973).

2. Ernst Troeltsch, *The Social Teachings of the Christian Churches* (New York: Harper, 1960); Max Weber, *The Sociology of Religion* (Boston: Beacon Press, 1963).

3. Frances Osterman Mischel, "A Shango Religious Group and the Problem of Prestige in Trinidadian Society," Ph.D. dissertation, Ohio State University, 1958.

4. Donald Hogg, "Jamaican Religions: A Study in Variations," Ph. D. dissertation, Yale University, 1964.

5. George Eaton Simpson, *Cult Music of Trinidad* (New York: Folkways Records and Service Corporation, 1961), FE 4478, 4.

6. Melville J. Herskovits and Frances S. Herskovits, *Trinidad Village* (New York: Alfred A. Knopf, 1947); George Eaton Simpson, *Religious Cults of the Caribbean: Trinidad, Jamaica and Haiti* (Rio Piedras, P.R.: Institute of Caribbean Studies, 1970).

7. Weber, *The Sociology of Religion*, 48.

8. That is, they do not need to rely on pilgrimages, offerings, and other fund-raising activities because they have enough money to maintain their own churches.

9. Weber, *The Sociology of Religion*, 66.

10. Jagdish Chandra Jha, "The Hindu Festival of Divali in the Caribbean," *Caribbean Quarterly* 22 (1976):53-65; Morton Klass, "East and West Indians: Cultural Complexity in Trinidad," *Annals of the New York Academy of Sciences* 83 (1959):855-861.

11. Andrew T. Carr, "A Rada Community in Trinidad," *Caribbean Quarterly* 3 (1953):35-54.

12. H. Richard Niebuhr, *The Social Sources of Denominationalism* (New York: Holt, Rinehart and Winston, 1929), 19-20.

13. Cf. Hyman Rodman, *Lower-Class Families: The Culture of Poverty in Negro Trinidad* (New York: Oxford University Press, 1971).

14. Simpson, *Religious Cults of the Caribbean*, 140.

15. Ioan M. Lewis, *Ecstatic Religion: An Anthropological Study of Spirit Possession and Shamanism* (Middlesex, Eng.: Penguin Books, 1971).

16. Simpson, *Religious Cults of the Caribbean*; Hogg, "Jamaican Religions: A Study in Variations."

17. Mischel, "A Shango Religious Group and the Problem of Prestige in Trinidadian Society."

18. Vittorio Lanternari, *The Religions of the Oppressed: A Study of Modern Messianic Cults* (New York: Alfred A. Knopf, 1963).

19. Alfrieta V. Parks, "The Conceptualization of Kinship Among the Spiritual Baptists of Trinidad," Ph.D. dissertation, Princeton University, 1981, 15-16.

20. Roger Bastide, *African Civilizations in the New World* (New York: Harper and Row, 1971), 29-30.

21. These are pseudonyms. Lloyd E. Braithwaite, "Stratification in Trinidad: A Preliminary Analysis," *Social and Economic Studies* 2 (1953):131, suggests that these organizations represent a bid for "respectability."

22. Dorothy C. Clement, "Shango: A Modernizing Cult in Trinidad Society," M.A. thesis, University of North Carolina at Chapel Hill, 1969, 25.

23. Richard N. Adams, *Energy and Structure: A Theory of Social Power* (Austin: University of Texas Press, 1975).

24. Herskovits and Herskovits, *Trinidad Village*, 343.

25. Ibid., 184.

26. Melville J. Herskovits, *The Myth of the Negro Past* (New York: Harper and Brothers, 1941), 222.

27. Many Baptist leaders did move their churches to less crowded areas, and, for that reason, older churches are not centrally located. By 1982, however, even areas around older Baptist churches had become heavily populated. Newer churches are almost always centrally located.

5. Leadership Decisions and Church Economics

1. Baptists recognize two types of missions. Most missions, like those described in this chapter, are primarily fund-raising activities. Sometimes, however, an individual will receive a vision in which he or she is instructed to "make a mission" to a distant village or even another island to warn people of an impending disaster. In the latter instance, no money is collected.

2. See Alfrieta V. Parks, "The Conceptualization of Kinship Among the Spiritual Baptists of Trinidad," Ph.D. dissertation, Princeton University, 1981, 88.

3. Many Baptists stated that visitors should fast on pilgrimage days, but few visitors seemed to conform to this expectation.

4. Many pilgrimages from the Curepe area are hosted by wealthy

churches in the South. This could have a homogenizing influence on church ritual, and, in time, a one-way pattern of diffusion from wealthy to poorer churches might come about.

5. Jeannette H. Henney, "Spirit-Possession Belief and Trance Behavior in Two Fundamentalist Groups in St. Vincent," in *Trance, Healing and Hallucination: Three Field Studies in Religious Experience* (New York: John Wiley and Sons, 1974).

Charles Gullick in "Shakers and Ecstasy," *New Fire* 9 (1971), 8, reports that among some Baptists in St. Vincent a group of about twenty "Shakers" (Spiritual Baptists) will hire a bus and take newly mourned individuals to services in other communities. It is unclear from Gullick's description whether or not Vincentian Shakers actually classify these travels as "pilgrimages."

6. Angelina Pollak-Eltz, "Shango-Kult und Shouter-Kirche auf Trinidad und Grenada," *Anthropos* 65 (1970):814-832.

7. However, they cannot refuse to receive pilgrims from other churches.

8. Melville J. Herskovits, *The Myth of the Negro Past* (New York: Harper and Brothers, 1941), 165, suggested that reciprocity and mutual aid are important components of African economic systems. He notes that almost all permanent groupings, other than the kinship unit, possess cooperative and even insurance features.

Leaders D. and W. claim that reciprocity in pilgrimage behavior is analogous in many ways to a Trinidadian institution known as '*susu.* The institution may have had its origins among the Yoruba of Nigeria and is also practiced on other West Indian islands and in the Bahamas. See Daniel J. Crowley, "American Credit Institutions of Yoruba Type," *Man* 53 (1953):80.

In Trinidad, '*susu* is said to make it possible for a person to carry on a systematic program of savings. A stated number of persons agree to deposit a certain sum each week with one of their number who undertakes to turn over the entire weekly collection to a different member of the group until all have received their "shares." An element of trust is involved as one gives in the hope that one will later receive back all of the money one has put into the system. Baptist leaders explain cooperation in pilgrimages in the same way. One allows other churches to visit in the hope that someday one's church will be received elsewhere and the church will reap the rewards of cooperation.

Also, it should be noted that Spiritual Baptists believe in the efficacy of numbers. The more people who attend a service, the more powerful the ritual. Pilgrimages involve more people than do regular services. This is seen as an advantage.

9. Thorstein Veblen, *The Theory of the Leisure Class* (Boston: Houghton Mifflin, 1973).
10. There is vast literature on this topic. See Helen Bagenstose Green, "Socialization Values in the Negro and East Indian Subcultures of Trinidad," Ph.D. dissertation, University of Connecticut, 1963; Walter Mischel, "Preference for Delayed Reinforcement: An Experimental Study of a Cultural Observation," *Journal of Abnormal and Social Psychology* 56 (1958):57-61.

Conclusions

1. Melville J. Herskovits and Frances S. Herskovits, *Trinidad Village* (New York: Alfred A. Knopf, 1947).
2. As Geoffrey Parrinder notes in *Religions in Africa* (New York: Praeger Publishers, 1969), 237, a characteristic of African religion is general tolerance that "allows people of different religions to live side by side, to learn from one another, and to prepare the way for religious dialogue."
3. Emile Durkheim, *Elementary Forms of the Religious Life* (London: Allen and Unwin, 1915).
4. Roger Bastide, *The African Religions of Brazil: Toward a Sociology of the Interpenetration of Civilizations* (Baltimore: Johns Hopkins University Press, 1978).
5. Michel Laguerre, "An Ecological Approach to Voodoo," *Freeing the Spirit* 3 (1974):12.
6. Cf. Stephen D. Glazier, *Spiritual Baptist Music of Trinidad* (New York: Folkways Record and Service Corporation, 1980), FE 4234, 5.
Alan Lomax in "The Homogeneity of African and Afro-American Musical Style," in *Afro-American Anthropology: Contemporary Perspectives*, ed. Norman W. Whitten and John F. Szwed (New York: Free Press, 1970), 189, discusses the various antiphonal forms in Afro-American music.
7. See Mary Douglas, *Natural Symbols: Explorations in Cosmology* (New York: Vintage, 1973), 84. Douglas's categories of "'grid" and "group" are potentially useful in the analysis of Baptist organizational forms.
8. George Eaton Simpson, *Cult Music of Trinidad* (New York: Folkways Record and Service Corporation, 1961), FE 4478, 4.
9. Michael Lieber, *Street Scenes: Afro-American Culture in Urban Trinidad* (Cambridge, Mass.: Schenkman, 1981), 109.
10. Ioan M. Lewis, *Ecstatic Religions: An Anthropological Study of Spirit Possession and Shamanism* (Middlesex, Eng.: Penguin Books, 1971).

11. Stephen D. Glazier, "Religion and Contemporary Religious Movements in the Caribbean: A Report," *Sociological Analysis* 41 (1980):181-183; Harold W. Turner, "New Religious Movements in the Caribbean," in *Afro-Caribbean Religions*, ed. Brian Gates (London: Ward Lock Educational, 1980), 49-57.

12. George Eaton Simpson, *Black Religions in the New World* (New York: Columbia University Press, 1978), 405.

Appendix: Shango Rites

1. George Eaton Simpson, *Religious Cults of the Caribbean: Trinidad, Jamaica and Haiti* (Rio Piedras, P.R.: Institute of Caribbean Studies, 1970).

2. Seth Leacock and Ruth Leacock, *Spirits of the Deep: A Study of an Afro-Brazilian Cult* (Garden City: Doubleday, 1972); Roger Bastide, *The African Religions of Brazil: Toward a Sociology of the Interpenetration of Civilizations* (Baltimore: Johns Hopkins University Press, 1978).

3. Frances Osterman Mischel, "A Shango Religious Group and the Problem of Prestige in Trinidadian Society," Ph.D. dissertation, Ohio State University, 1958; Dorothy Caye Clement, "Shango: A Modernizing Cult in Trinidadian Society," M.A. thesis, University of North Carolina at Chapel Hill, 1969; Simpson, *Religious Cults of the Caribbean*.

4. Similar to Seth and Ruth Leacock's description of the *ladainha* among the Batuque. See Leacock and Leacock, *Spirits of the Deep*, 95-96.

5. Frances Osterman Mischel, "African Powers in Trinidad: The Shango Cult," *Anthropological Quarterly* 30 (1957):45-59.

6. Chac-chacs are small, round, seed-filled calabashes to which handles have been attached. They play an important role in Trinidadian music. See Daniel J. Crowley, "The Shaki-Shaki in the Lesser Antilles," *Ethnomusicology* 2 (1958):112-115.

7. George Eaton Simpson, *Cult Music of Trinidad* (New York: Folkways Record and Service Corporation, 1961), FE 4478.

• Bibliography

Adams, Richard N. 1975. *Energy and Structure: A Theory of Social Power.* Austin: University of Texas Press.

Anthony, Michael. 1975. *Profile Trinidad: A Historical Survey from Discovery to 1900.* London: Macmillan-Caribbean.

Barth, Fredrik. 1959. *Political Leadership among the Swat Pathans.* London: Athlone Press.

Basch, Linda Green. 1978. "Working for the Yankee Dollar: The Impact of a Transnational Petroleum Company on Caribbean Class and Ethnic Relations." Ph.D. dissertation, New York University.

Bastide, Roger. 1971. *African Civilizations in the New World.* New York: Harper and Row.

————. 1978. *The African Religions of Brazil: Toward a Sociology of the Interpenetration of Civilizations.* Baltimore: Johns Hopkins University Press.

Beckford, James A. 1973. "Religious Organization." *Current Sociology* 21: 1-170.

Bee, Robert L. 1974. *Patterns and Processes: An Introduction to Anthropological Strategies for the Study of Sociocultural Change.* New York: Free Press.

Bourguignon, Erika, ed. 1973. *Religion, Altered States of Consciousness, and Social Change.* Columbus: Ohio State University Press.

Bowen, Marjorie. 1937. *Wrestling Jacob.* London: William Heinemann.

Brathwaite, Farley S. 1976. "Race and Class Differentials in Career (Value) Orientation." *Plural Societies* 7:17-31.

Braithwaite, Lloyd E. 1953. "Stratification in Trinidad: A Preliminary Analysis." *Social and Economic Studies* 2:5-175.

Brereton, Bridget. 1979. *Race Relations in Colonial Trinidad, 1870-1900.* New York: Cambridge University Press.

————. 1981. *A History of Modern Trinidad, 1783-1962.* London: William Heinemann.

Carr, Andrew T. 1953. "A Rada Community in Trinidad." *Caribbean Quarterly* 3:35-54.

Chevannes, Barry. 1978. "Revivalism: A Disappearing Religion." *Caribbean Quarterly* 24:1-17.

Clement, Dorothy Caye. 1969. "Shango: A Modernizing Cult in Trinidadian Society." M.A. thesis, University of North Carolina at Chapel Hill.

Crapanzano, Vincent, and Vivian Garrison, eds. 1977. *Case Studies in Spirit Possession*. New York: John Wiley.

Crowley, Daniel J. 1953. "American Credit Institutions of Yoruba Type." *Man* 53:80.

————. 1957. "Plural and Differential Acculturation in Trinidad." *American Anthropologist* 59:817-824.

————. 1958. "The Shaki-Shaki in the Lesser Antilles." *Ethnomusicology* 2:112-115.

Cumont, Franz. 1956. *Oriental Religions in Roman Paganism*. New York: Dover Press.

Desmangles, Leslie Gerald. 1977. "African Interpretations of the Christian Cross in Vodun." *Sociological Analysis* 38:13-24.

Douglas, Mary. 1973. *Natural Symbols: Explorations in Cosmology*. New York: Vintage.

Drake, St. Clair. 1975. "The African Diaspora in Pan-African Perspective." *Black Scholar* 7:2-13.

Durkheim, Emile. 1915. *Elementary Forms of the Religious Life*. London: Allen and Unwin.

Ennis, Philip H. 1967. "Ecstasy and Everyday Life." *Journal for the Scientific Study of Religion* 6:40-48.

Fabrega, Horacio, and Peter K. Manning. 1973. "An Integrated Theory of Disease: Ladino-Mestizo Views of Disease in the Chiapas Highlands." *Psychosomatic Medicine* 35:223-239.

Figueredo, Alfredo E., and Stephen D. Glazier. 1978. "A Revised Aboriginal Ethnohistory of Trinidad." In *Proceedings of the Seventh International Congress for the Study of Pre-Colombian Cultures in the Lesser Antilles*. Montreal: Centre des Recherches Caraibes. Pp. 259-262.

Foster, George. 1953. "Relationships Between Spanish and Spanish-American Folk Medicine." *Journal of American Folklore* 66:201-217.

Gates, Brian, ed. 1980. *Afro-Caribbean Religions*. London: Ward Lock Educational.

Glazier, Stephen D. 1980a. "Pentecostal Exorcism and Modernization in Trinidad." In *Perspectives on Pentecostalism: Case Studies from the Caribbean and Latin America*. S. D. Glazier, ed. Washington,

D.C.: University Press of America. Pp. 67-80.

———. 1980b. *Spiritual Baptist Music of Trinidad; Recorded in Trinidad by Stephen D. Glazier.* New York: Folkways Record and Service Corporation. FE 4234.

———. 1980c. "Religion and Contemporary Religious Movements in the Caribbean: A Report." *Sociological Analysis* 41:181-183.

———. 1980d. "Heterodoxy and Heteropraxy in the Spiritual Baptist Faith." *Journal of the Interdenominational Theological Center* 8:89-101.

Green, Helen Bagenstose. 1963. "Socialization Values in the Negro and East Indian Subcultures of Trinidad." Ph.D. dissertation, University of Connecticut.

Gullick, Charles. 1971. "Shakers and Ecstasy." *New Fire* 9:7-11.

Henney, Jeannette H. 1971. "The Shakers of St. Vincent: A Stable Religion." In *Religion, Altered States of Consciousness, and Social Change.* Erika Bourguignon, ed. Columbus: Ohio State University Press.

———. 1974. "Spirit-Possession Belief and Trance Behavior in Two Fundamentalist Groups in St. Vincent." In *Trance, Healing and Hallucination: Three Field Studies in Religious Experience.* Felicitas D. Goodman, Jeannette H. Henney, and Esther Pressel, eds. New York: John Wiley and Sons. Pp. 6-111.

Henry, Frances. 1965. "Social Stratification in an Afro-American Cult." *Anthropological Quarterly* 38:72-78.

Herskovits, Melville J. 1937. "African Gods and Catholic Saints in New World Negro Belief." *American Anthropologist* 39:635-643.

———. 1941. *The Myth of the Negro Past.* New York: Harper and Brothers.

———, and Frances S. Herskovits. 1947. *Trinidad Village.* New York: Alfred A.Knopf.

Hogg, Donald. 1964. "Jamaican Religions: A Study in Variations." Ph.D. dissertation, Yale University.

Horowitz, Michael, and Morton Klass. 1961. "The Martiniquian East Indian Cult of Maldevidian." *Social and Economic Studies* 10:93-100.

Imasogie, Osadolar. 1973. "African Traditional Religion and Christian Faith." *Review and Expositor* 70.

Jha, J.C. 1976. "The Hindu Festival of Divali in the Caribbean." *Caribbean Quarterly* 22:53-61.

Jules-Rosette, Bennetta. 1975. "Songs and Spirit: The Use of Songs in the Management of Ritual Contexts." *Africa* 45:150-160.

Klass, Morton. 1959. "East and West Indian: Cultural Complexity in Trinidad." *Annals of the New York Academy of Sciences* 83:855-861.

————. 1961. *East Indians in Trinidad: A Study of Cultural Persistence.* New York: Columbia University Press.

Laguerre, Michel. 1974. "An Ecological Approach to Voodoo." *Freeing the Spirit* 3:4-12.

Lanternari, Vittorio. 1963. *The Religions of the Oppressed: A Study of Modern Messianic Cults.* New York: Alfred A. Knopf.

Lawton, Samuel Miller. 1939. "Religious Life of South Carolina Coastal and Sea Island Negroes." Ph.D. dissertation, George Peabody College for Teachers.

Leacock, Seth, and Ruth Leacock. 1972. *Spirits of the Deep: A Study of an Afro-Brazilian Cult.* Garden City: Doubleday.

Lewis, Ioan M. 1971. *Ecstatic Religion: An Anthropological Study of Spirit Possession and Shamanism.* Middlesex, Eng.: Penguin Books.

Lieber, Michael. 1981. *Street Scenes: Afro-American Culture in Urban Trinidad.* Cambridge, Mass.: Schenkman Publishing Company.

Logan, Michael H. 1978. "Digestive Disorders and Plant Medicines in Highland Guatemala." In *Health and the Human Condition.* M. H. Logan and E. E. Hunt, Jr., eds. North Scituate, Mass.: Duxbury Press.

Malik, Yogendra Kuman. 1971. *East Indians in Trinidad: A Study in Minority Politics.* New York: Oxford University Press.

Malinowski, Bronislaw. 1935. *The Coral Gardens and Their Magic.* 2 vols. London: George Allen and Unwin.

Mischel, Frances Osterman. 1957. "African Powers in Trinidad: The Shango Cult." *Anthropological Quarterly* 30:45-59.

————. 1958. "A Shango Religious Group and the Problem of Prestige in Trinidadian Society." Ph.D. dissertation, Ohio State University.

————. 1959. "Faith Healing and Medical Practice in the Southern Caribbean." *Southwestern Journal of Anthropology* 15:407-417.

Mischel, Walter. 1958. "Preference for Delayed Reinforcement: An Experimental Study of a Cultural Observation." *Journal of Abnormal and Social Psychology* 56:57-61.

Newson, Linda A. 1976. *Aboriginal and Spanish Colonial Trinidad: A Study in Culture Contact.* New York: Academic Press.

Niebuhr, H. Richard. 1929. *The Social Sources of Denominationalism.* New York: Holt, Rinehart and Winston.

Niehoff, Arthur, and Juanita Niehoff. 1960. *East Indians in the West Indies.* Milwaukee: Milwaukee Public Museum Publications in Anthropology.

Oxxal, Ivan. 1971. *Race and Revolutionary Consciousness: A Documentary Interpretation of the 1970 Black Power Revolt in Trinidad.* Cambridge, Mass.: Schenkman Publishing Company.

Parks, Alfrieta V. 1981. "The Conceptualization of Kinship among the Spiritual Baptists of Trinidad." Ph.D. dissertation, Princeton University.

Parrinder, Geoffrey. 1969. *Religion in Africa.* New York: Praeger Publishers.

Pelto, Pertti J., and G. Pelto. 1975. "Intra-Cultural Diversity: Some Theoretical Issues." *American Ethnologist* 2:1-18.

Philpott, Stuart. 1973. *West Indian Migration: The Montserrat Case.* London: Athlone Press.

Pollak-Eltz, Angelina. 1970. "Shango-Kult und Shouter-Kirche auf Trinidad und Grenada." *Anthropos* 65:814-832.

Price, Richard, ed. 1979. *Maroon Societies: Rebel Slave Communities in the Americas.* Baltimore: Johns Hopkins University Press.

Raboteau, Albert J. 1978. *Slave Religions: The 'Invisible Institution' in the Antebellum South.* New York: Oxford University Press.

Ray, Benjamin C. 1976. *African Religions: Symbol, Ritual and Community.* Englewood Cliffs, N.J.: Prentice-Hall.

Rodman, Hyman. 1971. *Lower-Class Families: The Culture of Poverty in Negro Trinidad.* New York: Oxford University Press.

Ryan, Selwyn C. 1972. *Race and Nationalism in Trinidad and Tobago: A Study of Decolonization in a Multiracial Society.* Toronto: University of Toronto Press.

Sargant, William. 1974. *The Mind Possessed: A Physiology of Possession, Mysticism and Faith Healing.* Philadelphia: Lippincott.

Simpson, George Eaton. 1961. *Cult Music of Trinidad.* New York: Folkways Record and Service Corporation. FE 4478.

———. 1966. "Baptismal, 'Mourning' and 'Building' Ceremonies of the Shouters in Trinidad." *Journal of American Folklore* 79:537-550.

———. 1970. *Religious Cults of the Caribbean: Trinidad, Jamaica and Haiti.* Rio Piedras, P.R.: Institute of Caribbean Studies.

———. 1978. *Black Religions in the New World.* New York: Columbia University Press.

Smith, Michael Garfield. 1962. *Dark Puritan.* Kingston, Jamaica: Department of Extra-Mural Studies, University of the West Indies.

———. 1975. *Corporations and Society: The Social Anthropology of Collective Action.* Chicago: Aldine.

Sobel, Mechal. 1979. *Trabelin' On: The Slave Journey to an Afro-Baptist Faith.* Westport, Conn.: Greenwood Press.

Stewart, John O. 1976. "Mission and Leadership Among the 'Meriken' Baptists of Trinidad." In *Contributions to the Latin American Anthropology Group.* N. Whitten, ed. Pp. 17-25.

Troeltsch, Ernst. 1960. *The Social Teachings of the Christian Churches*. New York: Harper.

Tucker, Leonard. 1914. *"Glorious Liberty": The Story of a Hundred Years' Work of the Jamaica Baptist Mission*. London: The Baptist Missionary Society.

Underhill, Edward Bean. 1930. *The West Indies: Their Social and Religious Condition*. London: Jackson, Wolford and Hodder. (First published in 1862.)

Veblen, Thorstein. 1973. *The Theory of the Leisure Class*. Boston: Houghton Mifflin.

Wallace, Anthony F. C. 1961. *Culture and Personality*. New York: Random House.

Ward, Colleen, and Michael Beaubrun. 1979. "Trance Induction and Hallucination in Spiritual Baptist Mourning." *Journal of Psychological Anthropology* 2:479-488.

Watson, A. P., and Clifton H. Johnson, eds. 1969. *God Struck Me Dead: Religious Conversion Experiences and Autobiographies of Negro Ex-Slaves*. Philadelphia: Pilgrim Press.

Weber, Max. 1963. *The Sociology of Religion*. Boston: Beacon Press.

Whitten, Norman W., and John F. Szwed, eds. 1970. *Afro-American Anthropology: Contemporary Perspectives*. New York: Free Press.

Williams, Eric. 1946. *The Negro in the Caribbean*. Manchester, Eng.: Manchester University Press.

Wilson, Peter J. 1969. "Respectability and Reputation: A Suggestion for Caribbean Ethnology." *Man* 4:70-84.

———. 1973. *Crab Antics*. New Haven: Yale University Press.

Wong, Wesley. 1976. "Some Folk Medicinal Plants from Trinidad." *Economic Botany* 30:104-142.

Wood, Donald. 1968. *Trinidad in Transition: The Years after Slavery*. New York: Oxford University Press.

• Index

About the Author

Stephen D. Glazier is Visiting Assistant Professor at Trinity College, Hartford. His writings on religion include *Perspectives on Pentecostalism: Case Studies from the Caribbean and Latin America* (an edited volume) and articles in the *Journal for the Scientific Study of Religion*, the *Journal of Religious Thought*, and *Sociological Analysis*. In addition, he recorded *Spiritual Baptist Music of Trinidad*.